GU00984548

Radio Acting

Alan Beck

A & C Black • London

First published 1997
A & C Black (Publishers) Ltd,
35 Bedford Row, London WC1R 4JH

ISBN 0-7136-4631-4

© 1997 Alan Beck

Alan Beck has asserted his moral right to be identified as the author of this work.

All rights reserved.
No part of this publication may be reproduced in any form or by any means – graphic, electronic or mechanical, including photocopying, recording, taping or information storage and retrieval systems – without the prior permission in writing of the publishers.

A CIP catalogue record for this book is available from the British Library.

Typeset in 10½ on 12pt Sabon
Printed and bound in Great Britain by Biddles Ltd, Guildford, Surrey

Contents

To the memory of Derek Jarman (1942-1994)
film-maker, writer, saint.

Foreword

It is really rather remarkable that a book such as this has not been written before. Radio offers actors a vast amount of work; advertising on radio is a growth area and will offer more and more work for performers. So it is with great relish that one greets such a publication. This book will hopefully go some way to demystifying the process of both working and getting work on radio. I know how many still believe it is a closed shop.

Those of you who are fortunate to find such work will, I am sure, find the experience enjoyable and liberating. It is a cliché, but in a world that places more and more importance on style, fashion and the way we look, radio can offer you the chance to create characters that bear no relation to your own physicality. And having created these characters you bring enormous enjoyment to the millions who listen to BBC drama every week, and the many more millions who listen all over the world to the World Service productions. It is also incredibly hard work. You will need a fierce imagination and intelligence, coupled with instinct, to make creative leaps very fast, while collaborating with actors you may have only just met. Exhausting but exhilarating.

The listeners at home must not hear any of this hard work of course! Radio lives in the minds of its listeners. Each listener will create a different picture inspired by your performance and the writer's words. It is a remarkably intimate medium and listeners will often tell you that they remember details of radio plays much longer than work seen in the theatre and cinema. Radio plays demand levels of commitment and concentration beyond other media, and the listeners expect in return, first-class writing, performance and production.

Radio is also the premier medium for new writing. I would add one thing to Alan Beck's extensive advice, and encourage you all to read and see as much new drama as you can to keep up to date with trends, writers and ideas.

The BBC is very aware that it is the major producer of drama on radio in the world, and apart from a small number of independent production companies, the only producer in this country. We therefore take our role in training and supporting actors very seriously. The Radio Drama Company is central to this commitment and many of you might aspire to join it. Apart from the joy of having an acting company in the midst of us, the company provides a most valuable focus for the passing on of skills. Day in and day out, in studios and on location, you will see generous, experienced actors supporting and teaching newcomers. And being in the company gives new talent a chance to put these skills to use on a daily basis, to build on and consolidate them. The Radio Drama Company is probably one of the oldest, extant companies in the UK.

I hope that this book will encourage you to think about working in radio, encourage you to become a listener if you are not already one, and encourage more drama schools and colleges to include radio acting and radio drama in their curricula. If you are not getting the training you think you need, demand it!

Caroline Raphael
BBC Radio

Introduction

Radio acting requires:
- speed, commitment and accuracy.
- studio technique PLUS the other skills of acting.
- you 'lift it off the page' and create a bond with the listener.
- you do less, but do more with less.
- 'instant' results, often demanded.

'I'm dancing on radio': Sophie Tucker, in her cabaret act

Sophie Tucker joked about 'dancing on radio' as the easiest job going for an actor. Radio acting is a contradiction, creating character and movement from voice, in a blind medium. But working at the microphone is surprisingly physical and as much a matter of technique as film acting. Most obviously it breaks the unity of the actor; voice is parted from body and face, for what a character *says* is separated from what he or she *does*. Devoted audiences of radio drama for the nearly seventy-five years of its history have not suffered from this contradiction, getting as they say, 'the best pictures on radio'; and actors work with intense and creative energy to 'lift it off the page'.

So the message of this book is that the radio actor is not less of an actor. True, you do not memorize lines and you read from the script direct to the microphone. Rehearsal and production are fast, with one day in a BBC studio producing thirty minutes of a broadcast play. There is not the time as in stage rehearsal, say two to five weeks, to discover and build the character and ensemble. You work on these with intense concentration, back and forth from rehearsal to recording. Skill is not reduced to voice alone, for radio has its own 'body language' and movement. This, however, is not to deny the contradiction. Radio is not just an indirect medium, like film where the actor is not physically present with the audience, but it is the only blind medium.

Each part of the production chain is categorically different. For the radio actor, 'in the beginning was the word'; that is, he or she has to be committed to the text from the beginning and the character is revealed through language. Does that leave room for subtext and radio's body language? Absolutely yes, if you are to be expressive and convincing. You work without scenery, sometimes without getting hold of the sound props which are manipulated by studio technicians called 'Spot'. So, what of preparation and the sensory techniques pioneered by Stanislavski, to endow your play environment and fellow actors with meaning? You will discover that many of these techniques are available, essential to radio I believe, in which the actor's task is supremely one of imagination.

An acting manual cannot teach creativity or inject talent where none exists. There are neither rules nor a right way of acting. What my book offers is an insider's guide to the radio drama studio, making available to you the views and experiences of many practitioners, to whom I am deeply grateful for their input. I give you the range of choices from when you open the script, and as you prepare, build your character and perform. Above all, I hope you find here a full spectrum of radio skills, of radio technique at the microphone, including commercials, voice-overs and book readings. Without skills you cannot be expressive, believable and creative, though again I stress that these are choices and questions finally only you can bring to your performance.

When we say a radio actor has a good technique, we mean having a 'must-be-listened-to' and articulate voice, a skill in language, dialect, pace, pitch and rhythm. He or she is able to make the character live in their language, even to live in the pauses, and to 'keep in' the dialogue while others speak. Directors talk about avoiding the 'ping-pong' effect in radio dialogue, that switching abruptly from speaker to speaker, and about avoiding its 'talking-heads' nature which gives the listener the impression that the scene lives only from the neck up.

Because radio is blind, it takes skill to create the movement that goes appropriately with dialogue, even to give the listener the 'face' that goes with the words, in a series of 'sound pictures'. Scientists claim that in real-life talk, the visual accounts for 75% of the communication. Present-day acting in other media is also very visual and a lot of training goes into movement skills. Radio acting often means doing less, but creating more with it, working from the style and conventions of the play. It also means working on a succession of one-off productions, in what actors have always praised as the most creative of environments, with exciting new material reaching mass audiences, and often with the playwright present, in the case of new works.

Radio technique also means working effectively in the radio drama suite, and that is where Chapter 1 starts, with a tour of the studio set-up, leading to Chapter 2, production in the studio. There you learn of the two main production systems, 'rehearse-record', which moves back and forth between rehearsal and recording, like film and TV; and less frequently, 'rehearse-all-then-record' (at-a-run), where a whole play is rehearsed before beginning on the takes. Chapter 3 tells you of different radio directing styles, of the read-through, and the 'loss' of the director from the studio when recording. Chapter 4 teaches microphone work and the five positions at the microphone, along with perspective and movement within the sound picture 'frame'. Chapter 5 leads you to more creative work, especially in your radio body language or 'embodying' as I call it, and explains the speed, flexibility and commitment needed. Do you work on the character from the outside-in or inside-out? You'll probably use both pathways. In Chapter 6, you learn of the main aspects of the voice relating to radio: pitch, volume, breathing, tempo and rate, and voice qualities. Then how to work on dialect and relaxation. Chapter 7 aims at your creative interpretation: the key questions to ask yourself in preparation, profiting from your five senses, visualization without scenery, and using your partners effectively. I also ask 'what is bad radio acting?' In Chapter 8, I bring you into the market, radio commercials and audio books, and you hear the language of production through producers themselves. I also advise you on how to get started, and on your show reels and voice tapes.

Where the product is the voice, a radio actor can be physically any size and any look. 'Short fat actors can play long thin roles', it is said, and type casting happens less in radio. Reading this book will help you to extend your range. There is always a radio market for the actor with skill in dialect and the studio, and who can make fast and radical adjustments. What matters is the ability to take the listeners into the world of the characters through their language.

The United Kingdom is the outstanding employer of radio actors with its long tradition in the BBC, going back to the first radio production of 16th February, 1923, the quarrel scene from *Julius Caesar*; and the BBC richly merits its title of 'The National Theatre of the Air'. From the golden years come stars such as Marjorie Westbury, Carlton Hobbs and Tommy Handley; and radio directors are always able to assemble 'dream' casts for major classic productions. Now is an exciting time of diversity with growing independent drama production, which could rise further than the present 10% quota bought in by the BBC. It means radio actors meet all kinds of directors and in studios sometimes smaller than the BBC's, but so much has become possible through the magic of digital production.

Radio drama is a huge industry with a wonderful tradition, employing some 14,000 actors a year, and a turnover in fees of about £6 million, according to Equity. It has sometimes called itself the Cinderella of drama since television took over in popularity in the mid 1950s, and its plentifulness and constant high standards can make it seem familiar and securely available. But it needs protecting as never before in this new age of the BBC's Producer Choice and independents, because it is almost the most expensive item on radio, costing from £20,500 an hour for a Radio 4 play, down to £11,500 for some Radio 2 Light Entertainment. The statistical breakdown is as follows. Equity estimates that BBC Drama and Light Entertainment issued some 14,500 actors' contracts in 1996. Add to this the Radio Drama Company (RDC) of between sixteen and twenty, traditionally known as the 'Rep', and the World Service and BBC Education (a bi-media department). Fees earned by London contracts in the last financial year amounted to £3,012,000. The daily fee is £105 and the weekly salary for a member of the Radio Drama Company is £320 to £445, with students at £258.

The Archers has a regular cast of about 50 and a history of 720 characters over some forty years. Some local BBC stations produce drama, such as BBC Stoke-on-Trent's soap, *The Colcloughs*, though this has now completed its final episode, and Radio Kent, twice a year. BBC radio for schools supplies half an hour of drama for 7 to 12-year-olds, through 28 weeks a year. Unfortunately, in commercial radio the waves of radio drama have ebbed and flowed, such as Capital Radio's soap in the 1970s, and London's LBC Independent Radio Drama Productions (IRDP) until 1996, still fortunately surviving on the relaunched LBC. Then there are audio books and commercials on radio, and voice-overs for television commercials, documentaries and features. The Radio Advertising Bureau states commercial radio's revenues in 1995 amounted to £270.2 million, a growth of more than 20% from the previous year, and so is a booming market for actors.

Radio drama is famous for providing the most professional working conditions, and a camaraderie shared with trusted and skilled directors. You summon up intense, highly concentrated energy for one-, two- or three-day productions, and have the satisfaction that comes with the completed take and when everything is 'in the can'. Then you are broadcast to audiences of 2–500,000 or even over a million. Radio is generous about contracts, usually booking from within three weeks of the studio date, as agents will not commit their actors sooner. Weekend and day work suits availability, especially if an actor is in a stage run.

My book comes in the wake of professional voice training and manuals, especially by experts such as Cicely Berry and Patsy Rodenburg. I take up from the point where the voice is in readiness. You have developed so far that your voice is freed, and accurate and articulate in dialogue and dialect work. In Chapter 6, on voice, it is useful for me to go through some relevant aspects of voice production, but I concentrate on developing your voice further to the demands of the microphone and the studio. Being 'on' the words in radio most often means being more intimate, 'bringing it down', and judging, for example not just rhythms and timing, but even whether to use an inbreath or an outbreath. You direct the flow of energy in the voice stream in crucially different ways, depending on what I term the five positions at the microphone and on how 'opened out' the sound set is. The microphone cruelly exposes technique, imperfections of the vocal mechanism and insincerity.

The actor and actress of today work across all the media, from stage to screen, TV and video, and radio, and have to be able technicians. Two very different forms of acting are demanded by stage and screen. The stage energizes the actor much more by projection to the audience, in movement and often most of your work is in speaking. The camera often demands subtextual acting, psychology more than the words, a lot of 'face-making', keeping tightly within the frame, and often realistic 'invisible' acting.

Radio is a crossover of both but is truly the third form of acting. There is a complete focus on the words, the voice stream and dialogue, and the actor's energy must be expressively and economically channelled there. Without stage or screen costume, scenery and movement, you seem to do less, but that less is more. You will also discover that radio acting involves a lot of energetic and precise movement, including 'turns' from the waist, head moves, running, and shouting behind screens and into corners. It is not 'stand-and-deliver' acting. This third form of acting is also unique in that you can work simultaneously as both character and actor, as the studio gives that freedom. You can also communicate and signal to others as both. You benefit because most often your concentration is on one thing – the words – unless you have what are called moves. You 'make it real' in a substantially different way, acting in your mind's eye (or ear), a listener as well.

I have written this book for all who are developing their skills in radio drama, comedy, book-readings and voice-overs, in fact, for all actors, directors and production staff who work at the microphone. It is a first, because although radio drama has been on our airwaves since 1923, no training manual has ever before been published. I hope that all actors, whatever their *curriculum vitae*, will benefit, as an actor never stops training. Students usually complete a radio module and some conservatoires compete for the BBC Carlton Hobbs Award, allowing the winner a contract with the Radio Drama Company. It is worrying that only a very few schools appear to teach in an adequately-sized studio, affording enough space for microphone work and moves off. The result is that basic studio technique has to be learnt when at professional work and this is not an adequate situation. It is not enough merely to have made friends with the microphone and tried out an audition piece or two. Trainees are usually given many more hours with film and video. I hope my book will go some way to cover this gap. No matter how many training manuals are published, actors work from instinct and from experiences that have formed them and as such become finely tuned intuition. There is only so much teachers can do.

In an obituary to a wonderful actor and supreme radio performer, Sir Michael Hordern, the Radio 4 *Kaleidoscope* presenter Brian Sibley, who worked with him as the adapter of Tolkien, summarized him as 'an actor who brought very little intellectual baggage into the studio and didn't necessarily fully understand the emotional complications. He never said, "What's my motivation?"' As Sibley explains, 'Radio acting is telescoped. The actor has to respond much more immediately and switch on a performance.' Walter Matthau, after his first experience on radio with Fay Weldon's *The Hope in The Top of the World*, grumbled, 'Like all megalomaniacs I thought it would be nice for posterity, but radio is the kind of fake acting I don't like. Of course, all acting is fake.' Radio acting is fake only if you make it so for the listeners and I hope that with the help of this book you will be better able to act – and dance – on the radio.

General references to actors/actresses and to directors are sometimes in the male gender. Please understand these pronouns and possessives to refer equally to the feminine.

In putting this book together, I am touched again and again by the commitment, generosity and team-working of those involved, in the UK and Eire. They have handed over to me their accumulated wisdom and shown me their creativity in and out of the studio, and been patient and attentive through my interviews. I owe an enormous debt to them all and especially to Caroline Raphael, Jeremy Mortimer, Hamish Wilson, Patrick Rayner, David Lewis, Anna Sullivan and Brian Scott-Hughes for reading the book in draft, and giving me helpful (and improving) comments. Errors and omissions are my very own. I am indebted to a short guide circulated among members of the Radio Drama Company by Anthea Davies, studio manager, full of practical wisdom. My thanks also for support and advice to Liane Aukin, Robbie Burton-Saniger, Mike Bersin of Emap, Geoffrey Russell and Andrew Ingram of The Radio Advertising Bureau, Paul Fagin, David Hitchinson, Michael Earley, Christina Burns and Jon Page; and to Aileen La Tourette and Colin Finbow for permission to use excerpts from their outstanding plays. This book would not have been possible without my students at the University of Kent and the many days we have spent together in the radio drama studio. Final thanks to my editor Tesni Hollands, for being enthusiastic and helpful from the start of the project.

Chapter 1

Discover the Studio

There is a lot of technical information to be absorbed in this chapter. It is spaced out for easy reference to enable you to build up your knowledge step-by-step. Starting with a tour around the studio set-up, you will meet two sorts of production.

BBC production in a radio drama suite: the best equipped and dedicated solely to drama production.

Basic production in a smaller single studio: in a local BBC or commercial radio studio. Used mostly for a presenter and guests, this is called a talks studio. I have coined the term 'basic production', shortened sometimes to 'basic'. Basic also refers to production in colleges and schools with smaller resources.

THE STUDIO SUITE

The BBC radio drama suite is usually four rooms: a *live* studio, a *dead* room, the *control cubicle* and a *green room*. These are built for 'sound separation' so that sound does not penetrate through the walls.

The *live studio*: where most recording takes place. It is called live because sound reverberates off various surfaces and voices can be captured in all their interesting qualities. It is spacious enough for movement, as the actors make *moves* around the microphone. To give an idea of dimensions, the Pebble Mill Studio 3, in Birmingham, where *The Archers* is recorded, is 12 x 8 metres and 4 metres high. That is 40 x 26 feet and 13 feet high.

The *dead* studio or room: damps down sound reflections and is used for open-air scenes. The one in Birmingham is 2 x 3 metres, or 6 x 8 feet. Sometimes there is no separate dead room, but a *dead area*, as in the main studio in Broadcasting House.

The *control cubicle*: looks into the live studio through a long window. It is where dialogue, music and effects are mixed together. You find there the director and the production team. The mixing and balancing of voices, effects and music is done at the control panel, though increasingly this is left to post-production. The director talks to the actors in the studio through the *talkback*. In radio, producer and director are nearly always the same person.

The *green room*: a retiring room for actors during production and for child actors' chaperones. You do not stay in the studio if you are not needed.

The director has a production team of:

Panel SM (studio manager): at the control panel, in charge of the technical side.

PA (production assistant): who handles much of the production planning with the actors, and notes details of the recorded takes.

Grams SM or tapes: who cues and plays the effects (or FXs) on CDs, disk and cassette. (Grams is a term from when all the recorded FXs were on cumbersome 78s for gramophone playing).

Spot SM, one or more: who works with the actors in the studio, creating the Spot effects, such as opening and shutting doors, tea cups etc. Actors also do some of the Spot effects.

BASIC PRODUCTION

Basic is in two rooms: a *talks* studio, and *control cubicle*, separated by a window. This is the set-up in a local radio station or in a college or university radio station. But it can be even simpler. The control panel and grams may have to be in the same studio room along with the actors. Of course, it is difficult to separate production noise and instructions from the actors' dialogue. However, a lot can be achieved and there is the editing afterwards to pick up on problems before the finished product emerges. Many schools and colleges work in single-studio basic. As technology revolutionizes production, some BBC work is now in basic.

The basic team consists of actors, director, panel SM, grams, Spot (sometimes including actors) and PA.

Radio play production consists of three processes

Scripting and redrafting: worked on together by the playwright and the director/producer. The casting and contracts are done at this stage. The traditional BBC term was 'producer' and not 'director', but both are, as Jeremy Mortimer says, 'very separate jobs for the same person'.

Production in the studio with the actors: usually begun with a read-through before moving into the studio for rehearsals and recording. You work from 10.00 a.m. till 6.00 p.m. or even 7.00 p.m. in the BBC. Schedules are more flexible with independent production companies and actors with theatre commitments often work at weekends. One day in the studio usually equals half an hour of a broadcast play.

Post-production done by the panel SM and the director: the tapes are edited and more sounds are mixed in. They also complete a *trail*, or radio advertisement that lasts a minute or less, and is broadcast during the week leading up to the play.

No matter how you work, in BBC or basic, a great deal of preparation has to be done before actors and director join in the studio. As all radio directors emphasize, time in the studio is at a premium. Every unit is costed and is becoming more and more expensive.

Around the studio suite

Now comes the tour of the studio suite. When you walk into the live studio, you first notice that it has clearly different areas and these offer contrasting sound environments. Walls and floor are divided into different surfaces with various forms of panelling.

One section of the floor is wooden planks, the rest carpeted. This carpet can be rolled back for the concrete underneath. The walls have different horizontal panelling of padded cloth. Heavy double curtains can be drawn across the middle. There are screens moving easily on wheels. One side of each screen has a hard, reflective surface (called *live* or *bright*); and the other side has deep cloth panelling providing an absorbent surface (called *dead*). They measure approx. 2 metres high by 1 metre wide (6 x 3ft). These furnishings, along with framed doors and cupboards on wheels, and steps, offer different combinations of acoustics, the basics for sound sets.

Technicians talk about these different acoustics created in various regions of the studio as being *bright* (reflective, returning sound echoes) and *lively* (ditto), *boxy* (enclosed, small and echoey) and *dead* (absorbing sound). A live studio like this offers seven basic areas.

Surfaces absorb or reflect sound.

Combining these creates different acoustics: *bright/live, boxy* and *dead*.

We hear either direct sounds, sound waves directly to our ears; or indirect sounds, which are sound waves reflected back off various surfaces before they come to us. Direct and indirect sounds help to create the acoustic.

There is also a flight of stairs with perhaps fourteen steps. Each step is in triplicate because side-by-side lie carpet, wooden and concrete surfaces. Running or walking up-and-down these yields different results. They may lead to a balcony, also useful for acting on a higher level, some three metres (10ft) up. In a side wall is a practical sink with one cold tap. A true professional will always run the tap water a little, first thing, so as to maintain a constant flow with no failure when eventually it is needed. Twenty or so flagstones are stored in a corner and will be used in say, a Shakespeare play. There are about a dozen microphone stands and a lot of cables, neatly arranged. There is also a round table with chairs, partly for production, but it can be used for the read-through and for script discussions. The narrator character sometimes sits at the table.

A long soundproof window along one wall connects with the control cubicle in which the director and SM are just visible sitting at the control panel. Actors often give an inquiring glance at the glass. Instructions come from the director there via a microphone and to a loudspeaker in the studio. This is called the talkback. Directors give their notes on the talkback, unless they have moved into the studio, alongside the actors for more complex and perhaps more tactful conferring. Other loudspeakers in the studio can also be used for playing back the takes that have just been recorded and other material from the control cubicle. Directors do not do this often, but when they do, they say to the actors, '*I'll let you have it on the playback*'. You will learn about all this in detail in Chapter 3, Production in the studio. It is a golden rule for most directors not to play anything back to the actor, because it is heard out of context and invariably results in a retake.

You go through a door into the dead room and within it you see the gravel walk, permanently built-in, and some bigger stones. These are for Spot and suited to outdoor scenes. The dead room is

Studio with actor at stereo pair microphone and Spot working behind screens.

much smaller and heavily padded inside with panels. Since it muffles all sounds and absorbs them into the padding, there is little or no sound reflection. You get an unnatural sense when you talk in there because you do not get a return to your ears of reflections from your own speech. A studio manager described it to me as like 'talking into a feather bed'. It can be claustrophobic to work for long periods in the dead room as you cannot see outside. But there is a window panel that can be opened up if necessary. A video system sometimes allows the director to check actors' positions there. It can also operate in the main studio.

Think of the radio drama suite operating like a radio play factory. It is easier to grasp the technical points by seeing it as a manufacturing process in the broadcasting chain. Actors and Spot direct their work to the microphones in the two studios (live or dead). All this is fed back through the sound channels (you see the cables) into the cubicle. Each sound channel has a different source microphone. There it is mixed digitally (usually) with other sounds from other channels within the cubicle, coming from recorded CDs, cassettes and rarely now, vinyl records (FXs or grams).

The actors at the studio microphones could be characters in a street scene, but the street atmosphere (atmos) is mixed in within the cubicle, further down the manufacturing line. That street atmos must be separated from the dialogue and the actors do not get to hear it in the studio. Some actors might ask to hear an atmos, or the director requests it, so that they can pitch their voices against it. The main technical work on all these separate channels is done at the control panel or sound mixing desk. Two processes are involved here: mixing the different sound channels; and setting them each at the correct level for loudness, against each other or balancing one another. Increasingly often, the atmos is added in post-production, further down the broadcasting chain. The end result is the broadcast play.

Sound channels feed into the control panel.

Sound channel inputs are mixed and balanced.

Now it is time to step further into the control cubicle and look at the control panel, a long mixing desk. It should be familiar to you from theatre sound technology or you may have seen the mixing console at a radio station. Each of the sound channels is separately here, a long perpendicular slot, and there may be as many as forty. Each is operated by a slider called the fader (potentiometer or 'pot' for short). They operate in pairs for stereo.

The fader brings in the sound channel (raises the volume) or takes it out again (reduces the volume till silence). Hence the expressions: to *fade in* or *fade up* (bring in and increase the volume), and to *fade out* or *fade down* (reduce the volume until silence or 'black'), or 'pot it', if it is the fastest sort of fade. The fader is also termed 'open' or 'shut'. When you fade out till silence, you *fade to black*, though for some that is a TV, not a radio term. So when the fader is open on the control panel, anything on that particular microphone can be heard in the control cubicle. Be warned that as the microphone does not have a red light on top like the TV camera, you have to guard your tongue and not say anything you might regret later. As production opens on each sequence of script, the control cubicle tests out the levels on each microphone with the actors and balances the input. This is called *taking levels*, as in '*let's take some for level*', and actors have to give some lines of script on cue. Sometimes it requires detailed work and this is one of the technical aspects of radio acting, rather like standing in position on stage while lighting levels are adjusted. It is time-consuming and you have to be patient.

The final result of all this mixing work on the control panel is a digital recording; or if on analogue tape, it is relayed to a reel-to-reel tape machine, which records all the takes for the master tape of the play. The PA's job includes noting all the different takes, their times and their labelling, with comments. The next process after production is post-production editing with further mixing. Then the play is ready for broadcast.

Stereo/mono and the sound picture

Stereo/mono: BBC production is in stereo, rarely in mono. Stereo uses two microphones, a *stereo* or *crossed pair*. These two microphones are usually on the same stand or there is a double microphone. Mono uses one.

Blocking and moves: *blocking* is your positioning and you *stand to your mark* (a theatre and film term). *Moves* are around the microphone.

The sound background: in the scene this is the *acoustic* or *ambient* sound or *atmos*. It could be traffic, a crowd, or for example, what we perceive as ambient in a sitting room. Even silences are different in radio drama.

Perspective: this is where you are placed in the sound picture. It is a combination of how near or far you are to the microphone, in relation to your fellow actors and how that input is mixed at the control panel.

> **Production is either in stereo or in mono.**
>
> **As an actor, you work either to a single microphone (mono) or to a stereo pair.**
>
> **BBC drama production is in stereo, even on AM or medium wave (mono).**
>
> **Basic production is mostly in mono.**

The difference is in the sound picture the listener gets. If you are listening on Radio 4 longwave, a mono play is two-dimensional – you can only hear how far apart the characters are, and how close. It is as if they are placed along a single line. So they are either very near to each other, as for a love scene or in a car, or quite close, in a living room, or further apart, as across a field. Only one radio speaker is needed for mono listening.

Stereo carries a three-dimensional sound picture. You hear the characters spread out across the left and right speakers in the 'sound stage', the area between the speakers for the listener. You get a sense of the characters moving around within the sound picture, in a three-dimensional way. Somebody comes in through the kitchen door on the back left, say, and approaches over to the sink on the near right. The production has to keep this consistency of 'architecture'. You can also hear a car or a jetplane moving across left-to-right, or right-to-left. To be technical, there are five positions across the stereo speakers that you hear as a listener: hard left, left centre, centre, right centre and hard right. The skill is in creating a composite of stereo sound and filling 'the hole in the middle' between the two stereo speakers. It has to be admitted that few people listen in such ideal conditions.

Acting in mono or stereo makes an enormous difference for the actor as regards his or her position or blocking. If you are in mono, what matters is how far or near you are to the microphone. Mono production in BBC, up to the mid-1970s, meant the actors were in a circle around a central microphone. Any actor could make his 'approach' or entrance from any point within 360 degrees of the microphone field, and stand anywhere in relation to the fellow actors.

But in stereo, for correct perspective, you have to be positioned spatially: both near or far, and also left and right. For example, if you have a love scene on the sofa, you have to be both close to the microphone (for intimacy), and at the same point together, probably centrally. Your partner cannot be hard right while you are hard left! Listeners would be jolted by the inconsistency, because the perspective is wrong. (A confused listener is a lost listener.) So the stereo positioning or blocking has to be correct both as to left-and-right, and to distance from the microphone. This gets more complicated when there are moves to be made. Positions can be indicated with masking tape on the studio floor.

The microphone and blocking

Field: Microphones have a field, which is their working area. Step out of this and you are heard indistinctly or distantly. In mono, you go *into the dead*. In stereo, you go *out of phase*.

Direction: Some microphones are 'omnidirectional', or live all the way round, and others are 'figure-of-eight'. Most have a precise working area, often a semicircle for the stereo pair. See Appendix III for microphone diagrams.

Centre: You need to know where the centre (the front) is in both stereo and mono. You'll often see the technicians counting at various positions around the microphone to check it.

As an actor, you work to a variety of microphones, but do not be put off by this. The SM shows you the area – the field and the centre, and how far round you can move before you are *off mike*. As you go out of the microphone field, your voice becomes quieter and disappears. You will be shown the edge of the field which is best marked on the studio floor. If you turn off the mike, it can have the effect of the character moving suddenly away, or vanishing, *down a hole in the floor* as directors put it. Precision with your moves is the rule, especially in stereo at the edge of the field.

> There are two strict warnings:
>
> ✗ NEVER TOUCH THE MICROPHONE!
>
> ✗ NEVER BLOW INTO THE MICROPHONE!

You might have seen someone tapping the microphone to check if it is operational, or blowing into it. This is bad practice. Professional microphones are expensive, BBC ones can be as much as £1,000, and the Neumann is nearly £2,000, so there are strict rules for their care. You are told which microphones are 'faded up'. It can be a problem, if you want to communicate with the control cubicle, but Chapter 4 tells you how to do this.

To work out your position in relation to the microphone:

> Treat the microphone as if it were a human ear or the person to whom you are talking.
>
> When you drop your voice, move a bit closer.
>
> When you raise your voice, lean back, or turn your head away from the microphone, or across.

There are five positions for dialogue at the microphone

These five positions are not standard for every production though they are usual. I have invented the term, the five positions, for teaching purposes (it is not in use in the BBC). Surprisingly perhaps, you are often not told where to position yourself, except perhaps in relation to the other actors.

Position 1: You are as close to the microphone as possible without distortion. This is used for being intimate, for interior thoughts, or 'interiorizing' as I call it. Being so close, sometimes you speak across the microphone, and not directly into it. Your SM will usually advise you.

Position 2: Your mouth is about half an arm's length from the microphone. This is for intimate dialogue, for personal secrets shared, for intrigue in the plot, a conspirators' scene, say, and asides.

Position 3: This is for ordinary conversation. Position 3 is what actors use most often. You should be near enough to the microphone to stretch out your arm and reach it with your wrist. If voices get a bit raised in heated dialogue, you move back until the microphone is in fingertip reach. If it gets louder, you go back another six inches if in mono, and if in stereo, you make a turn aside. You will find your director may ask for more intensity and less volume.

Position 4: Your positions further away than position 3 are called *moves*. You could be coming in the door, going over to a drinks cabinet, exiting down stairs, opening the window.

Position 5: This is further away again, coming down the studio stairs, on the studio balcony, or behind a screen. This opens out the action to further away. Stereo has turned the radio studio into a busier place with more moves and a more interesting sound stage.

Here is an end of scene, using all five positions.

1. **MOTHER:** Is that all you have to say to her? It's your baby she's having!
   [Position 3 – ordinary conversation]
2. **HUSBAND:** [going] I can't stand this. I'm off to the pub.
   [Position 4 moving to 5, exiting off mike and travelling on the line]
3. **FX:** DOOR SLAMS
   [Spot operator with Spot door]
4. **MOTHER:** What are you going to do, love?
   [Position 2 – intimacy]
5. **WIFE:** [Crying]
   [Position one – her crying in 'close-up']
   FADE TO BLACK
   [Fade out to silence for end of scene]

The sound set and Spot

To realize the correct sound acoustic for each radio scene, Spot constructs a *set*. This set is the studio part of the acoustic. Technicians build in the studio with screens, carpets or planks on the floor, and curtains. That sort of set may be enough and 'read' sufficiently well in itself, for example, for a living room, a kitchen, a hallway. Otherwise, for scenes on the street, in a car, or a cathedral, or a factory, an atmos is added 'on top' in the control cubicle. Digital technology is increasingly taking over the functions of the set, creating 'artificial' or virtual environments by processing or treating the voice. **Note:** An acoustic is the way your voice sounds in a particular place, such as a phonebox or the Albert Hall.

Actors work in these sets for each sequence of the script. The simplest set is merely reading to a microphone. The problem for the actor is that this studio set offers no visual clues to represent the scripted scene and it looks nothing like its final sound picture when broadcast. What you see are microphones, screens, curtains, panels on the side walls, with carpet, wooden planks or a concrete floor. You have to depend entirely on your imagination and there are suggestions on how you trigger it in Chapter 7. As director Brian Scott-Hughes puts it, 'The guy opposite you in jeans is really the Pope!'

Then there is the Spot equipment such as the famous radio drama door and the sash window, cups and saucers on a low table perhaps. The mixing of the acoustic to the scene is done within the control cubicle, from digital processing, effects CDs, grams and cassettes. But the performing actor rarely hears this background 'layer' of the atmos, such as traffic, seagulls, a crowd and rain. Cubicle may play you a short excerpt of it before the rehearsal of the scene begins, to help you with a taster. The reason you never hear the background, or only hear it very low, is that otherwise the sounds would be recorded twice, once via the speech microphones as well as via the cubicle and this would sound impossibly odd.

Sometimes, an acoustic is played into the studio to be picked up by the microphones. It could be a TV playing, a home stereo or a train announcement. The technical term for this is *foldback* and it is played through on loudspeakers. You also hear of a third type of acoustic called *neutral* and this means the sort that gives no particular background to the voice. Again, you will learn about this in detail in Chapter 4.

More warnings:

✗ NEVER MOVE ANY PART OF THE SET. IT HAS PRECISE POSITIONS.

✗ BE CAREFUL STEPPING OVER CABLES.

Working with Spot

Spot technicians work the sound props because this requires expert timing, it is a technical skill, and both hands must be free of the script. Nowadays, many actors prefer to do as much as possible themselves, and you will always find Spot friendly and supportive.

Some Spot effects are: tea cup clinking, glass and bottle, key rattling, coins, newspaper, letter opening, letter writing, boiling kettle and making tea, washing up, cutting bread, playing chess, torturing and executions (chopping vegetables), door opening and closing, door bell, locks, drawing curtains, footsteps (in the gravel box) and 'walking' on various surfaces (slabs of concrete, wooden planks, up and down studio stairs, on and off wooden box – all with Spot shoes suitable to the character), lawnmower, hedge clippers, hair drier, clicking on and off TV and radio, DIY tools, typewriter and computer keyboard, cash register and 'fighting' with period weapons for Shakespeare and historical novels.

Spot also wears *your* 'clothes' and 'shoes', that will 'read' (are convincing) over the air. Obvious examples are period costumes (rustling skirts, armour), but you wear them too, and a note with your script may ask actresses, for example, to arrive in long skirts. In comedy sketches for the Radio Light Entertainments Department, Spot can be very busy.

You can appreciate that to do your own effects would be distracting for you, so you leave it mostly to the 'techies' as on stage and film. Another technical factor is that many Spot effects have to be recorded in their own set, behind screens, with their own microphones and their levels balanced against the voices. Some Spot effects are sharp, high-level sounds with what is called 'attack' in their first impact (hammering, electric machines, chopping). You have to do some effects yourself because only you can make them sound authentic, such as drinking, eating, choking and kissing (though you have to kiss your co-actor and not just your arm). If you have energetic physical action to do (swimming, rowing, climbing, wrestling, fighting, digging, horse-riding, herding animals), you will learn in rehearsal to take the lead and let Spot fill in the details.

Spot are a performance in themselves, bizarrely comic, so do not

Actor in 'moves off' descending while Spot creates 'steps for another character

be distracted by them and always respect their work. If they are at your microphone, they are intimately close to you and they may have to get hold of you to guide your moves, pushing and pulling. You will notice that they have to be precise about the Spot props, so that a cup cannot be exchanged for a glass, and a wine glass sounds different from an ordinary drinking glass, and so also for period plays. Obviously there is a lot that they can fake or 'cheat' as it is called with substitutes and sometimes because these sound more effective. It is the sound not the studio reality that matters. When you drink as a character, you could be given a hot liquid because, believe it or not, hot and cold drinks sound differently. Prunella Scales in the monologue *The Box of Chocolates* tried nibbling other tit-bits, because she did not want to eat so many chocolates. But these were not believable and so she redid the thirty-minute play with chocolates, most successfully. Even cups and glasses have got to be precisely what they are in the script. There used to be a strict BBC demarkation that actors could not do Spot. You will find a further discussion on how you work with Spot in Chapter 5.

Cue lights

RED is for recording and GREEN is the cue for 'go'.
Cue lights are set up around the studio in a number of places because they are used for the beginning of every take and for a variety of cues within the take. In a complicated sequence, the director could cue separately: Spot, two particular actors, then another group of actors and more Spot or moves. The lights are on the studio walls and also on separate stands, that look rather like waist-high ashtrays, and can be moved around. You are directed what your particular cue is and you have to make sure you can see the light from your blocking position and that you mark your cues in your script.

This completes your first tour around the radio drama suite. You have learnt some basics here in radio play manufacture and the next three chapters guide you through the actor in production. You will probably need to refer back to this section to refresh your memory, so check all the key points highlighted in bold, and the warning instructions with the symbol ✗. Production is very much a stop-and-start process and it is essential for you to know what is going on in the control cubicle.

WHAT THE RADIO PLAY SCRIPT LOOKS LIKE

When you look at a professional radio play script, you notice how the production details are clearly annotated and that everything is numbered. It is much simpler than a camera script for TV. All the words the actor does *not* speak are underlined. Particular directions for the actors are in lower case and underlined within brackets. For example, [angrily] and [with rising tension]. Production directions for the control cubicle or for Spot look like this:

FX: FADE UP SEA WAVES AND SEAGULLS

That is, they are underlined (often), with upper-case capitals and marked FX. Each character's individual speeches and the FXs are numbered from the top of the page. This numbering begins afresh at 1 on every new page. It is an essential way for everybody to locate points in the production script. For example, the director might say, 'We'll begin again from the middle of 5 on page 33, at, "There were witnesses to that, inspector?".'
You have to mark up your script with all sorts of notes, suggestions

for which follow here, and in the appendix (see page 162). The sign FX does not differentiate between Spot (in the studio) and FXs in the control cubicle. So the FX atmos above comes from what is termed 'grams' or 'tapes' (meaning CDs mixed in by the grams operator in the cubicle). Don't forget your pencil!

Here is an excerpt from a scene:

1. MANIAC:	So I see you want my evidence now.
2. FX:	MANIAC RUSTLES PAPERS.
3. SERGEANT:	Please calm yourself. Don't open that window!
4. FX:	FRANTIC STRUGGLE. WINDOW OPENED. TRAFFIC ATMOS.
5. MANIAC:	Here I go—!

At 2 and 4, the FX comes from Spot. At 4, the TRAFFIC ATMOS (meaning atmosphere or acoustic) is from the grams operator, mixing in from CD. At 4 the struggle is done with the actors and their moves, but Spot could help especially if it is difficult for the actors to hold their scripts for this business.

What you can do

You now have enough information to start *listening professionally* to radio plays. Try to listen with concentration, on good equipment and stereo speakers, and at a high volume. You will not be able to do this for every play, obviously, but you need to develop this professional listening – necessary to all radio play practitioners. Buy a stereo Walkman for more convenient listening.

> **Recognize different atmoses (or sound backgrounds): living room, roadside, inside the car, factory, neutral, inside the head (thoughts or interiorizing).**

> **Identify the difference between Spot effects (in the studio) and acoustic FXs ('laid on' in the control cubicle). See how the sound picture is constructed in layers.**

> **Discover perspective – how the characters are blocked and move around within the sound picture. And how the sound picture has three dimensions in stereo.**

> **Identify each actor's five positions at the microphone.**

Chapter 2

Production in the Studio

You have now covered the basics of studio set-up, microphones, Spot and the sound set and acoustics, and had your first tour of the drama suite. In this chapter we will look at the studio in action: working in production.

Two production systems: *Rehearse-record*, and *Rehearse-all-then-record* or *at-a-run*.

More studio equipment to get to know: headphones, cueing, foldback.

Production is by the *schedule*, which lists each sequence and its production time.

Begin with a read-through, then move on to rehearsals and recording.

Mark up your script precisely with instructions (notes) as you go along.

Penny Gold, director:
Some directors rehearse till the actor gives the right performance and then they record it. But as in film, you rehearse till you are nearly there and then you record it. That's the first time it 'goes'.

Two production systems:

Rehearse-record

This is by far the most frequently used system. Each section of the play is rehearsed and then recorded. Studio production moves from one sound set to another, sometimes recording consecutively all the scenes requiring that one set before moving to the next. Obviously the script makes its own logic, as do the technical demands of constructing the acoustic of the sound scenes, and even the availability of actors. Microphones have to be moved, often with screens and cables, and Spot effects are sorted out. Sometimes the storyline is broken up and the production is disjointed, recording against the narrative flow, out of sequence. But radio usually manages to keep to the sequence of the scenes, as in the script. You do not often get to record the opening scene first or if so, it is often re-recorded later.

Rehearse-record is the method of TV and film. So working actors, who do their 'jobbing' across the media, acquire the skills to cope with the discontinuities. But it challenges you as a radio actor if you have to face a crucial finale scene, for example, early in recording.

Nicola Pagett prefers rehearse-record: 'Look, as an actor, you are either a marathon runner or a sprinter. With short spurts, it's easier to concentrate.' For Jonathan Taffler, 'Rehearse-record requires real preparation, you need to be centered on the character. There are disadvantages. One-and-a-half days into a three-day production, you suddenly realize who the character is, and half your performance is already in the can.'

Graham Padden has worked in rehearse-record only and thinks 'it's sometimes helpful to chop around the play out of sequence. Though commonly, the scenes are still done in a fairly chronological way. I remember in the play *And When You Sleep You Remind Me Of Dead*, I had scenes of dialogue with a psychiatrist and then flashbacks to past experiences. It would have been extremely difficult to record this in sequence, at-a-run. We broke it down and got through all the psychiatrist scenes in a block.'

Production of most radio plays is rehearse-record.

All the scenes in one sound set can be recorded together.

The play storyline is sometimes broken up.

Steve Nallon, playwright and actor:
The number of times the rehearsal is better and fresher than the recording! You wish the tape had been running. There's something about reading it for the first time.

Director Martin Jenkins sometimes records the second half of the play first, so that when the actors come round to the first half, as Christian Rodska says, 'It's all geared in. And the audience get a real integrated feel of the play through its first half.' Pam Brighton, director in Belfast, tries 'as hard as possible not to work out of sequence and I work pretty quickly when I get going. I also record rehearsals.' Tessa Worsley likes rehearse-record 'in big chunks, as when the director says, "We'll do those three scenes again – you know what you are doing," and that is very satisfying.'

It is useful here to contrast the stage process, rehearsal-to-performance, which divides out into three sections. Firstly, read-through to the point of 'laying down the book', and from there to the dress rehearsal, and then the run itself. Stage production clearly distinguishes between the rehearsing actor who is then transformed into the performing actor. The actor has to make his or her transfer from the rehearsal 'in here' to the 'out there', in front of the theatre audience. The radio actor has the advantage of rehearsing and performing in the same set and in the studio.

The range of tasks in the radio rehearsal is obviously less, including the technical. So much time in rehearsals in theatre, for example, is spent in backtracking and validating previous decisions, and also checking the actors' memories. Radio goes in short sprints, without the need for run-throughs to shape and reshape the whole.

Basic rules for rehearsal apply across all the media. As an actor, you have to fuse with the author's lines. You have to listen to your scene partners and communicate with them, and from them to the audience. You have to work at various levels at the same time – for radio, your microphone positions, your head focus, moves, as well as all the other demands of the script. In the even more compressed rehearsal time for radio, comparatively the shortest in relation to the product, you have to balance letting results happen versus too much striving on your part. Finally, you have to realize the character within the demands of rehearsal and recording. The emotions and the 'reality' of the character have to be switched on and off, but they have also to be stimulated and controlled.

Rehearse-all-then-record, or at-a-run

This is the process of the more 'stage-type' radio director who prefers to record in the second half of the production. The whole play is rehearsed and built, scene by scene, and that leaves the recording to the last – always with a touch of danger, because it risks running against time. It will be in the afternoon, in the case of a single day's production, or the second day, in the case of two.

The benefit of the 'at-a-run' method is that it enables the total architecture of the play to be built and so the actors realize the trajectory or 'spine' of their characters. To use Stanislavskian terms, the actor can move fluidly from each of his objectives to the next, and develop his through-line of action. This system can also benefit some types of plays, such as certain Thirty-minute plays, two-handers, monologues and adaptations of one-hander or smaller cast stage plays. In the old days of live-performance mono, production had to be simpler for what were called 'oners' (once-offs) and 'at-a-run' was the rule. After rehearsal, they went out live, right through the play without a break and it really had to be the best performance. Actors tell of exciting re-writes during broadcast, with new endings rushed in, when tragedy turns to joy.

At-a-run is also confined by the size of the studio. Production moves from one sound set to another, and the studio can only accommodate a small number of sets simultaneously, and building a new set takes up necessary scheduled time. At-a-run means going back and forward between a small number of sound sets.

For actor Jonathan Taffler, 'recording at-a-run is much better for more theatrical plays. Personally, I think it is a mistake to use this method with plays that have shorter themes. Actors enjoy recording at-a-run. Ideally, I like to have an overnight to think further, before committing to tape. The only directors I know who use this method are Richard Whortley and Jane Morgan. She usually leaves recording to the last day. When we were doing *The Jenny Wagon*, it was four days and I felt I'd been through so much development that it was like four weeks in rehearsal.'

Diana Bishop finds this process 'a great benefit if you're working on a play which builds. It's wonderful for the actor to be given a run at it, to keep up a pitch of emotion. You get the frisson of excitement, like the stage. When I was working with Jane Morgan, I had to read a very emotional letter towards the end of the play. I was as nervous waiting for that scene as if I was in the stage wings, my heart was thumping. I get the adrenalin rush only in "at-a-run" productions.'

Christian Rodska cites an unusual example of Alan Plater's *Sky Hooks* transferred from the stage at the end of its run to radio with the same cast. 'We couldn't have done it any other way and we didn't need to hold scripts.' He also gives examples of long takes, especially with director Martin Jenkins. 'He likes to work us like mad and leave things to the end to record, at times. In Sartre's *Les Mains Sales* (*The Assassins*), we had a 72-page take, because we were running out of time. It set a real flow on it and made it like the theatre.' Working with director Tony Cliff on a Thirty-minute play, 'going by the schedule, technically, we could finish early. He says, "Why don't we do the whole thing again?" In that final run, it would take off. It's useful too for the control cubicle, because they can almost edit the play while doing it.'

James Aubrey sees some disadvantages. 'At-a-run takes a long time to set up and it's structured like a stage play, as much as possible. Actors find moving from one set to another is taxing.' He also cites advantages. 'You catch the power and rhythms of the others. Listening to the actors in the preceding scenes, and you are coming in four minutes later, say, it's thrilling and like standing in the wings. While in the control cubicle, you catch sight of them running around like dervishes.' Lastly, to return to memories of old mono days, director Jane Morgan tells of a nightmare broadcast when 'the actors started fluffing on page one and could not get themselves out of it'. On another occasion 'a loudspeaker packed up, and the actors had to keep on broadcasting, while gazing at the men in white coats who came in and took it away, and replaced it'.

Rehearse-all-then-record or _at-a-run_ separates recording and rehearsals, leaving recording for the last part of production.

This system demands a concentration and continuity similar to stage performance.

You have more opportunity to build your character.

At-a-run is limited to a small number of sound sets.

Don't be a script rustler!

One of the greatest dangers in the studio is what is called script rustling, or script flapping – making a noise with your script that is picked up by the microphone. Let's deal with it right away, with its causes and solutions. The problems are: having the script in hand nearly all the time, turning over the pages, your moves, and acting in constricted sets. Then there are super-sensitive microphones. The cubicle team have to be sharply on the lookout for script rustlers.

Here are the voices of the experienced. Director Hilary Norrish says, 'at times you can't understand why an actor is being so "scripty". It's because they are inexperienced.' For Kerry Shale, 'either people get it right away or not'. Graham Padden laments 'it always seems to happen at a crucial point in the recording.' There is also the problem of the photocopy paper itself. Actors of long experience complain of the BBC change-over from the quiet old Roneo 'blotting-paper' in the 1960s. (BBC scripts are not now photocopied but printed on wood-free paper, a quite expensive business.) 'Actors tear apart scripts more. If you're playing at a desk, and there's six pages, you can lay them all out in front of you.'

Actors sometimes have to deal with heavier scripts and in narrow sets. You can be very close to the microphone and this makes the turn-over a real difficulty. The blocking may be tight, with you and others packed around the microphone. It is not just your blocking, but you could be more exposed because of the acoustic. It might be 'neutral' – there is nothing in the sound picture but you and your voice could be close.

Anthea Davies, BBC Studio Manager, comments, 'All I can say is, it isn't impossible, I know this simply from observation. Many actors and actresses never make a sound with their scripts, including a good number of those of riper years, whose eyesight may be short, whose ears may not hear quiet sounds, and whose hands may sometimes tremble. It's all a matter of practice and believing that you can do it.'

Don't become a script rustler! Be disciplined. Bend up the bottom right corner. Do not let two or three pages vibrate against each other.

Write in your cues at the top and bottom for difficult turn-overs. Use a highlighter pen. Split up your script into easy-handling wads. Take out the staple and hold only the pages you need.

Use your eyes and watch the most experienced members of the cast. Copy them.

Your script should never come between your face and the microphone. Don't mask your voice.

Don't put your script in a hardbacked folder as it masks other voices from the microphone. It's clumsier and heavier to hold. Don't hit the microphone or its stand or lead with your script.

In the BBC, do not turn 'off' from the microphone to make your page turn-over, holding it elaborately out at arm's length. Rustle is then picked up at the edge of the stereo picture. Your head also makes an unnecessary turn and this can catch you out when you come in on cue.

When you turn your pages, don't rustle when other actors are speaking. It's easy to think that if you're not speaking, the microphone can't hear you.

More studio equipment to know and use

Headphones

Sometimes called *cans* because their old originals were said to look like two condensed-milk cans stuck on each ear. They are either conventional or the new infra-red (cordless) technology. You wear headphones:

For telephone calls: You are on a separate microphone from the other caller, so you can hear the dialogue through the cans. See below for further details.

To hear some other part of the scene: when it cannot be audible in your set in the studio. Also when you play against a background, as a storm. Sometimes you record your character's 'thoughts' over dialogue, playing 'on top of yourself'.

As narrator and for single-voice readings: only infrequently.

There is one problem in working on cans. You hear all the studio output, including yourself. So do not be put off by 'hearing yourself back'. The older-style headphones plug into the wall and connect by a long lead that can impede movement. They have no separate volume control on them. They also plug into the table when you are narrator, for single-voice readings. Infra-red headphones require no lead and are fed by an infra-red signal from radiators near the ceiling. You can see these in all BBC drama suites, usually at corners. Anthea Davies reassures actors, 'There is no truth in the notion that the infra-red beam will focus on your brain and microwave it!' These cans are rather heavy, but they give free movement and have their own volume controls. They come with a small receiver and battery which hangs on your belt. One director warned, 'actors usually hate cans'.

The panel operator should not send signals at high volume down the cans to the actors as this could damage your ears. If it happens, Anthea Davies says to 'take the cans off at once to protect your ears, and put in a strong complaint.' The problem is if actors wear cans when they should not, to listen in to what is going on at the control panel, then anything could come through, at any level, without warning. Anthea gives the example of SMs who could be dubbing gunshots or selecting music at very high level.

Cue lights *and cueing*

Actor in studio (jokily):
Cue light not working? Let's do it without a light – let's face it, lights are so formal.

You should always be able to see your cue lights. Make sure that you understand the instructions for your particular cue, given to you by the director or SM. This can be complicated as there are usually a number of cues for separate entrances and actions, including Spot. GREEN is for go and you react immediately.

As Anthea Davies says, 'The SM will allow for people who are slower and quicker. Slowness or quickness doesn't seem to depend on age, youth, experience or whatever, as far as I can see, it just seems to be something you're born with.'

The big mistake is to hesitate when the green cue comes on, as this can throw the whole timing of the scene or the sequence. With so many small takes, sometimes down to one word, cueing is a crucial skill. A radio actor lives on the cue lights. He knows how to breathe in when the GREEN comes on. From the point of view of the cubicle, and the panel operator, some FX must be faded in before the actor's cue, and it is essential the actor hits it at the precise moment.

There are two types of cue lights:

Master cues: all the cues are lit when the SM hits the button. Everybody sees the cues.

Individual cues: these are for each actor, or small groups of actors, or for a crowd, or for Spot.

Here is an example of multiple cueing from a *French Revolution* play sequence. The tumbrel is on the way to the guillotine, with the hero passing in front of his accusers. It is even more complicated for the studio because the tumbrel is pushed in a circle past four microphone pairs. The master cue is for the crowd, dispersed round the studio, doing background shouts. Second individual cue is for Spot and the tumbrel is got moving. Third cue is for the hero, with a microphone round his neck, and he gives his own thoughts heavenward. Fourth cue is for the group of accusers he passes.

All this set has to be arranged, positions worked out, and individual cues given. The sequence starts fine, and then there could be a hitch and it restarts but from halfway down the page, not the top. There could be new cue lights given out. So the message to you, the actor, is to be attentive to cue instructions, to keep the cue in eyeline and always check in case of doubt. And to mark up all cues, and new cues, on your script.

Be warned! Cue lights for the new take can come very quickly and without warning after the rehearsal. There is so much going on in the cubicle that often, no more notice is given. The SM or director will say over the talkback, 'Right, ready for the cue lights everybody.' Then the cue could come on immediately, or there could be a pause of any length, or so it seems to the actors, and then suddenly, the cue light. Wearying as this is, you have to be ready to give your best. And that is professionalism. To repeat, it is most important to mark up your cues in your script because it is very easy to get confused. If you are hidden by part of the set, and cannot see the cue light, you can get a visual cue.

In the days of mono, when plays went out live, or were recorded on disk as whole scenes, the cue lights were used a lot. A rapid flashing of the green light was a crucial signal from the director to quicken the pace. The technical term for this was 'quick flicks' and they were inserted between scenes, after the fade to black and before the next scene was faded in. While 'slow flicks' meant to slow the pace. Think of the concentration needed from the mono actor in these 'oners' as they were called (live plays).

Fraser Kerr remembered when *Morning Story* went out live and 'the director gave you lots of flicks. Every paragraph was timed and the stop-watch was in evidence constantly. If you were a few seconds over – fast flicks on green. Or slow – slow flicks. In transmission, you tended to go too fast usually. My worst experience was with a John Masefield ballad – the poet refused to let us cut a single stanza, almost impossible to get it in on time. David Davis the director was flicking all the time. We got it in on the second. In the studio, with the green light flashing, I thought it was like a train!'

Independent director Turan Ali says, 'I like cue lights, I use them a lot, although inexperienced actors don't speak as soon as they see the green light – they even wait till it goes out! Sometimes I need a cue to govern the length of a pause and if I'm adding something in post-production. It can seem like a slap in the face for a skilled actor but it can be difficult for him to time a pause to the technical requirements of production and what is going on in the control cubicle. The reason is I could be adding on later a ticking clock or music.'

Talkback

This is the device that relays instructions from the director and SM in the control cubicle into the studio, via a loudspeaker.

The biggest problem for the actor is that there is a constant flow of instructions from the talkback, but it is one-way. You have to realize that the talkback is activated by a button which is held down. During this, you cannot be heard, even though you want to make a point or two. You have to be patient and wait for the talk-back message to finish. There may be a delay or gap in the middle of what the director says and, for example, he might be checking something with a technician in the cubicle. You have to wait for him to finish, and to take his finger off the 'key' button, but he does want confirmation from you, or a question. Sometimes a wave 'yes' from you is sufficient.

If you want to reply, you have to speak via the nearest microphone that is faded up. You may not know which this is, because the SM fades the microphones up and down for various reasons. But by hand-signals from you, or from him, you can sort out which microphone to approach. Above all, do not shout into this microphone, just talk normally. Also you should direct your voice towards this microphone, even though your eyeline wants to go to the cubicle window. You will not be heard otherwise. It is also tempting to approach the cubicle window and do what directors call the 'goldfish routine', or to go for the microphone nearest it. Do not be tempted. You want the nearest microphone they fade up. The normal rule is to 'stay put' and remember that the director has to come through three doors to get into the studio.

Programme

This comes through the same loudspeakers into the studio. *Programme* is the term for the output of the studio and you can only hear it when all the studio microphones are faded out. You hear programme sometimes – music or FX or pre-recorded narration – which precedes the sequence about to be taken. This then cuts out and it is your warning that the microphones are being faded up and the cue light is coming. Programme may not be fed to the loudspeaker because of what is called *howlround*.

You recognize this by an ear-splitting shriek. The cause of howlround is a signal feeding from the loudspeaker into the microphone, and going round and round till it builds in two or three seconds. The only solution for the SM is to cut the programme.

The problem for the actor is that he may need some of the preceding sequence, before his take, to make sense of his cue. He has rehearsed this before the take. But when it comes to the take itself, the SM does not feed through programme. There is only the cue light.

Foldback

Foldback is fed into the studio through a different speaker, which will be placed where needed. It is picked up by the microphones because it is needed to simulate a record-player (a teenager in a bedroom, for example), or a home radio or TV (in a living room or kitchen) or PA announcements (in a train station, an airport or a factory), which in real life are heard via a loudspeaker, or bombing in the Blitz. Only by arranging the foldback in this way does it fit into the sound picture convincingly.

The speaker is placed on the live side of the microphones. The levels will sound probably too quiet to you, but that is because the panel operator is balancing them via the microphones. Director David Hitchinson of BBC World Service makes much more use of foldback. 'I place the actor aurally in the location in which he is performing, as a church with its echo or a nightclub, or a telephone conversation, and this helps to build the reality for the actor, with the right mood, and improve the quality of performance. It's a matter of overcoming the technical problem of foldback in the studio.' Gunshot is one of the most difficult problems for radio because it is a sudden high-volume sound. To represent gunshot, the programme loudspeaker is placed on the dead side of the microphone, usually, and you will notice that the shot never sounds loud enough. But you can't have everything.

Atmos

You rarely get to hear your *atmos*. That is the atmosphere of the sound picture in which you are placed. If you ask the SM, he will play a sample back to you through the programme loudspeaker. But it cannot be at the level required for the background to your voice in the take. It is time-consuming to attempt this and it would need pre-recording it specially. So, frequently you do not know what you are playing against. It is a bit like the old film studio technique of acting against a back-projection, like countryside or on horseback, or in a car. It is over to you to create everything, as you are not acting within the play environment. It could be that the atmos is being laid on later in post-production. Chapter 7 suggests some techniques to help your imagination.

These are essentials you should get to know but do not expect to grasp them all in your first studio production. After all, if you were training as a radio journalist in a BBC local station, you would have three months to get on top of the technology. Director Hamish Wilson says that he would not expect an actor to know the technical differences of microphones, 'and not a U89 from a U87. That's down to the director and Studio Manager. But if an actor wants to learn that, I'm content. I've always said to all cast members, and it is my philosophy, that if you wish to sit in the cubicle, please do so. Young actors have been eager to do that.'

Chapter 3

Actor and Director

Hamish Wilson, director:
It's not to do with your voice, it's to do with acting. If it's right in your head, your heart and your belly, then what comes out of your mouth has to be right. If I can get the performances, I'll sort out the nuts and bolts.

How to team-work with your director

Know all the script and do your study. Arrive well on time. Be a 'quick study', as it is called in theatre.

Respond quickly and flexibly to director's notes. Be ready to change accent and characterisation.

Mark up cues and notes on your script carefully. Your director will notice!

Indicate you have heard his or her note over the talkback when it comes from the control cubicle. Be attentive.

Keep consistent with the original take and stay in place at the end of the take, till 'flickered out'.

Get more knowledge and confidence about studio technology. You are part of a team.

Martin Jenkins, director (over the talkback for a first take):
*Good luck, everybody, **please**!* (A famous note, much prized by actors.)

Nicola Pagett, actress:
Radio directors, I find, are not so much different from other media, as they are very expert. You have to trust them enormously, they are very rarely wrong.

What an actor wants from a radio director

To be a guide on the type of play, and on the character's voice, style and underlying attitudes.

To give feedback on good and bad choices, and making adjustments.

To interpret and communicate, to bring instinct and experience, both in the cubicle and the studio, and with the playwright (if present).

To give specific notes and clear leadership, especially on style, pace, mood and meaning.

To experiment within time constraints and to draw all together as a team.

To explain technical aspects of production, often with the Studio Manager.

To bring life, coherence and believability to every script including the ordinary.

To keep to a tight schedule and budget rehearsal time, and to arbitrate on questions of play detail and logic.

In film it is said, there are as many styles as there are directors. Radio directors seem to have less individual renown. They receive little publicity and are rarely interviewed, even on Radio 4's *Kaleidoscope*. Who – outside the 'business' – can name a radio director? In fact, radio directors, or producers as they are still sometimes called, enjoy high reputations with actors, firstly because of the expert training the BBC supplies along with the technical team. There are many house styles within the BBC and room for individual creativity among the thirty, approximately, directors in the UK; and then there are independent directors, most of whom have been in the BBC. Radio directing has not suffered from the endemic faults of British stage directing: poverty of training and experience. Just as on stage, radio directors tend to specialize. It is a mark of prestige to direct radio Shakespeare, the best-known playwrights such as Tom Stoppard and Alan Ayckbourn, and contemporary plays at the Royal Court, the Royal National and the Royal Shakespeare Company; and to work on Radio 3 and the Monday Play. With stage and novel adaptations, the radio director has a double task: to define and interpret creatively the conventions and period style of both the script and the original work; as well as dealing with larger and more starry casts.

For radio directors production is 'all-or-nothing' within one, two or three days in a studio that is enclosed and creative as a work place. A good working relationship with a radio director promises more bookings for actors, and with shorter production time together it is less likely that human and working relations will buckle under pressure. So radio is without many of the tensions of stage rehearsal, of laying down the book and the withdrawal of the director on the first night.

In this chapter, I offer you a wide range of opinions from actors about directors so that you can gain an insight into how diversely they work. The most important issues are:

Which director's notes are effective?

How much time should the director spend in the studio?

Read-through or not?

DIRECTING STYLES

Let's begin with directing styles. Diana Bishop finds 'most directors trust me and I trust them for choosing me because I'll do the work they want. They'll feel free to tell me if I've done anything wrong.' Actor Graham Padden described the forty radio plays he has done in Birmingham under only two directors as 'a unique relationship that you couldn't have in other media. There's a team that get together, the majority have worked with that director before.'

Andrew Sachs praised Glyn Dearman who 'has done most of my plays and I found John Gibson, who died in the 1960s, inspiring and very strong. I find many other directors don't think freshly and are too bogged down in the conventions of radio drama. Take the famous car door. To anyone who has not heard radio, they'd listen and say, "What the hell is that?" Genuinely fresh thinking is hard to come by. Directors don't hound the actor enough, they accept the second-rate as good.'

One actor wondered 'what feedback a director gets and what goes on in those BBC boards when they discuss the plays in detail with the bosses. After all, a stage play gets reviews and you all read them. Take someone like stage director Ronald Eyre, I remember him looking just flayed by a bad reception in the papers. Eyre turned down the position of Head of BBC Radio Drama because, he told me, he was temperamentally unsuited to institutional life and the grind of successive productions.'

The most frequent complaint from actors is over-rehearsing. Actors feel that they have been brought too far before the take and that the most creative moments have then been lost. This is obviously more dangerous in the 'at-a-run' production system, if in a one-day production, for example, rehearsals have taken up all the morning. Another complaint, and this applies to directors in all media, is the very rare 'show-and-tell' director who, instead of giving creative and motivating notes, 'performs' the lines for the radio actor, imposing emphases and intonation. This is humiliating for actors, forced to copy by rote what they have not discovered for themselves.

From my observation, the director has to answer frequent queries about facts and about the 'logic' of the scene. Of course this involves interpretation, but so many actors come up with 'I need to get the logic of this,' or 'I need the motivation here,' or 'Is that move of mine logical? Shouldn't I be over there by now?' or 'I've forgotten who that Greta you mentioned is; she's your niece or something?' Within the short production span, it is difficult for actors to discover and retain all the given circumstances, story and character biographies. They do not 'live' in the script long enough for everything to be at their fingertips as it would be in the weeks of exploration in stage rehearsals that provide the luxury of committing it to memory and doing run-throughs. Nervousness and concentration can lead to some quite obvious questions being asked. So the sensible advice is: try not to ask careless questions but do *ask*.

Director's notes

The director gives notes face-to-face in the studio and over the talkback when in the cubicle.

There is not much opportunity for privacy, everybody hears your notes.

The best notes are specific and creative.

Christian Rodska, actor:
You might disagree with a director's main notes on your part. Directors are only human.

An actor (overheard):
In BH I never get lectured on the play, thank heavens – none of that Open University circle squatting on the floor.

Carole Boyd (Linda Snell of *The Archers*) does not like 'too many notes because the actor becomes confused' and 'notes imply changes all the time which make you go round in circles until by day three of production, for example, you're lost'. On the other hand there is 'the director who does not give enough notes, relies on the actors' talent and the technicians, and takes a back seat, and you want to say: "Why did you bother to come in?" The actors are aware that something is wrong, try to pull it together and that's not their job.' Moir Leslie (vicar Janet Fisher in *The Archers*) condemns the sort who is 'a producer rather than a director, who casts well and works with the playwright, but is not helpful with the performance.'

James Aubrey comments: 'If you're doing well, the director doesn't give you notes, that's just like the theatre. Director Glyn Dearman, for example, was an actor himself and is sympathetic. Some directors just aren't, they are too academic, they explain ideas at great length. It's not really a help when you are standing there, with teeth, tongue and lungs. They could save time and heartbreak. Better to say, "Speak up, luvvie, and don't splash the mike".'

Matthew Morgan mentioned a director who 'gives line readings and that's hellish. Though occasionally it makes sense. But to be given stresses constantly is distressing and counter-productive, especially if it goes against your logic and you don't have time to absorb the detail. And you have to try to hit it all the time.' Jonathan Taffler was inspired by Jane Morgan: 'Three words from her and you change your entire performance around.' Angela Pleasence agrees. 'She looks at me and I know what the note is. Radio directors are so skilful, we have a short-cut coding system.'

Matthew Morgan relates an actors' joke concerning one particular BBC director. 'His notes always seemed to be "Brighter, faster, much mentally faster". This was because he blocked actors very close to the microphone and liked them to talk "incredibly quietly and very fast". I warned a friend being directed by him for the first time to take it easy on the first two openings and wait for him to interrupt. It all happened as I said. That can wear you down! The same director also gives you notes for the entire scene in one go – that's a mistake, it gets confusing.' Matthew comments on other directors. 'Clive Brill is perfect, he's quite tough. A note of his can turn me up and down, and it may be just "more energy". Glyn Dearman is very concerned with blocking and position, then he'll leave you to it.'

Anna Gilbert comments, 'The director has to notice the slightest thing I do off beam, like something not in line with accent or a word mispronounced or stressed wrongly. He has to have a good boredom threshold, especially for take after take.' Jilly Bond found, 'Martin Jenkins demanded incredible intensity and wanted me to use the tiniest voice, and to channel that intensity. He'd say, "Less volume," and even, "No volume at all," and he was right!' Director David Hitchinson posts background material to the actors. 'For the play *Nuremberg*, I sourced the material and edited it, and sent out quite a lot of briefing. As a director I have to be a catalyst not a dictator, and the firm idea I have has to go into the casting. When I first started, I tended to over-note, and in *Mrs Warren's Profession*, after I talked for five minutes, Timothy Bateson suggested, "If we do it first, we might get some of it right, and then we can talk!" I have to allow time to grow, if we have time. People in theatre might find us lazy, but it's much more difficult in radio to find the correct buzz words.'

Diana Bishop remembered the oddest note she'd heard. 'It was not to me but a girl and this was what came over the talkback: "As though you had torn your life into little pieces and it had fallen around your ears." It would have been more helpful if he had said "sadder" or "slow".' Another director is reputed to have said, 'I want you to think, "What colour is my entrance?"'

Director and cubicle

There is a divide here between directors who spend more time in the control cubicle and those who get into the studio more, even between takes. As James Aubrey summarizes, 'Some directors spend 90% of their time in the studio and only disappear for recording. Some stay in the box the whole time.' Steve Nallon explains why. 'The director has to sit in the control cubicle, because ultimately he does not get the proper impression of what you're doing if he watches you. You may lift an eyebrow, and that could mislead him, and it won't "read" on the air.' Anna Gilbert feels that 'the director has to have antennae that bore through the cubicle window.' For Matthew Morgan, 'Clive Brill listens in the cubicle and does not come in for the first rehearsal. He roughly blocks it and then wanders off.' Diana Bishop prefers, 'if I'm doing a reading, and I'm alone in the studio, for the director to come into the studio a lot. That's because I've worked so much in theatre.'

In a highly entertaining lecture she gave on BBC2, Sian Phillips remembered producer John Griffiths in Cardiff from the days of mono. 'He would shake his fist at us. He would leap up from the control cubicle as we went out live. At the worst, he would come into the studio and we would hear a series of muffled thuds as he went through each of the sound doors to us. He was the only person who could stamp on his toe! He would interpose his furious self between you and the microphone. He would also do on-the-air editing, it was most dangerous – ripping pages out of the script and throwing them on the floor. (That was in the days when the BBC could afford proper thick paper.)'

Read-through

It brings actors and technicians together.

It allows timing and script adjustments.

You can get an idea of others' performances.

But it can slow down a production and it may not suit the play's style or the director's system of production.

Read-through is the first reading aloud of the script by the gathered cast and with the technicians present. It usually takes place in the conference room, or the office, and occasionally in the green room, but rarely in the studio. It is what is called 'dry', without sound and music effects. There are directors who dispense with the read-through altogether and begin with notes to the cast instead. Others regard it as indispensable, and begin shaping scene structures and character voices right away. The PA can time the script sequences more exactly. Sometimes cuts to the script are decided, particularly to shape the play to time. Often there are word and phrase changes for readability and character consistency. If the playwright is present, he or she does the redrafting. It is over to you to contribute and get in immediately with any difficulties you spot, and that is another good reason for being well acquainted with the script beforehand.

Directors now discover how this cast sounds working together, as choosing them was a process completed, at most, only three weeks before. There might be unwelcome changes in the interim. Some actors offer nearly a complete performance right away, often that is encouraged, though in theatre it is called 'results-playing' and can be intimidating. This is especially useful in comedy and in genre plays, and in 'classic' acting, typically adaptations from the stage. But, just occasionally, it might indicate a problem for the director, tipping him off to an individual's desire to control the other actors and himself.

The read-through for any production is surrounded by private rituals, fears and hopes – ask any actor. Director and cast face up to their task together. Some or all are strangers to each other. Here are directors' views first.

Read-through: for directors

For Caroline Raphael, 'The read-through is essential and it cannot be an actor's performance, you build from it. Points of discussion come up, but I must work from the practical not from theory.'

Patrick Rayner says, 'I expect my actors to arrive with a more or less finished performance and then we work on that.' Penny Gold explains that 'radio is not like the stage read-through, where it's common for actors to keep their cards to their chest. The director must have a sense right away of where his actors are coming from. There isn't the chance in radio production to have runs of scenes, there's only time to get the sense of the play. After the read-through, things suddenly change and you are into the dynamics of rehearse-record. That's particularly so with comedies, where scenes can go on too long. So an actor should have done a lot beforehand, with homework study, and thought a lot, and keep an open mind.'

Hilary Norrish's purpose is, 'you can pick up the acting problems at the read-through, that's why we have them.'

Sally Avens (originally Radio 5) is more dubious. 'I don't expect much more from the read-through than to look at the play technically, to consider entrances and something about performance. You don't have the luxury of tearing a character to pieces and building it up again.' While for Turan Ali, independent director, 'More and more, I don't bother with the read-through. It's a waste of time. If the actors have prepared properly and you've spoken to the actors before – which doesn't happen often enough – they know your aims. Beginning at ten in the morning, with a read-through you've lost the best part of an hour – that's an eighth of the working day. (You work till six.) So I go for rehearse-record of the chunk of script I want to do first. That gives the actor a bearing on what you want and the rehearsal gives you a sense of where the actors are. Actors can find the read-through a waste of time and they don't bat an eyelid if you say there's none. Some say the read-through gives the actors a sense of timing, that's spurious, for me.'

Jonathan Taffler gives an actor's approach. 'Most actors who do a lot of radio do commit to the read-through. It's the one chance you get to see the whole play and how your performance fits into the whole. Other actors can work off you. It is one of the longest chunks of rehearsal time you get. If you are seriously off-beam, you discover this from your director and not just before a take. Actors should not keep their performances to themselves, you need to be flexible, to adjust quickly. That's the big rule – I always tell student actors this when I'm teaching.' For David Holt, 'it [read-through] allows the actors to try out what they want with the script. It gives the technical people a chance to hear it, though they don't always listen in.'

Christian Rodska cannot remember a production without a read-through. 'Most actors dislike them and feel nervous. You are almost expected to give a performance. At odd times in his notes, a director will say, "God, I didn't see it like that." If you get told that your interpretation is not justified, you go off at lunchtime, and instead of drinking, you think like hell.' Graham Padden finds, 'most of us expect basically what the actor will offer in performance. The rest of the exercise is to tune and develop. It's common at the end for the director to say, "He's a bigger man", "It's quite physical", "Make him older" or "heavier". Curious how these notes are often a physical idea.' Tessa Worsley hopes that financial cuts do not lead to the loss of the read-through because 'it lets you see the kind of person you're working with and you don't have to be looking at them in the studio.' James Aubrey remembers, 'I've seen actors fight to restore cuts. But what if a one-hour play is running fifteen minutes over?'

Steve Nallon finds in comedy, 'the first reading is always the best reading. Often the director says, "I wish I'd taken that."' Director Jane Morgan remembered the whole cast wept in response to Ronald Pickup's monologue from *The Road to Rocio*, in a scene set in the allied forces' graveyard. While Alaistair McGowan finds, 'some older comedy actors don't appear at their best. But on microphone, they dredge it up, it might sound melodramatic then. However, hearing the broadcast, it's just right.'

Read-through: for playwrights

Wally K Daly speaks for playwrights. 'When you attend the read-through, you leave go of your baby. As I listen to the actors, I realize the voices in my head haven't quite said it well enough. In the old days, I used to knock on the green-room door, sit down and say hello. But now I learn, I look for what the scene is about. So I look out for what I think is the germ at the heart of the scene, see whether it drives the play forward and earns its keep in the play. In my first play, *Whistling Willy*, I knew every voice, every pause, I was so dogmatic. I told director Martin Jenkins where he had gone wrong. He took me into the corridor and said, "You are the skeleton and you have to allow the studio to put on the flesh." I never say anything unless it's constructive and I allow other talents to give to the piece. I often say, particularly if there are child actors, "This is the only opportunity for the writer to hear what he has written. If you can read it as written, you'll be a great help to me."'

The 'loss' of the director

During the take, when recording is in progress, the radio director works in the control cubicle, sitting beside his panel SM at the control panel. The director has rehearsed with the actors in the studio and then moves to the control room to start the recording process: trying the actors' voices for levels, auditioning Spot effects, further rehearsing and then takes. Now communication is only through the talkback into the studio. At odd times, the director moves back in for notes, person-to-person. But in BBC suites, that means going through two or three doors and down a corridor, and so there may not be time or energy for this.

There is another similarity here with the stage actor. He suffers the 'loss' of his stage director from the first night. That can be traumatic for some professionals, especially if they have self-projected their director into the role of 'nurturing parent'. (See Stephen Aaron's *Stage Fright* for an illuminating discussion of this.) The radio actor has to cope with the 'loss' of or 'separation' from his director who must sit apart in the control cubicle. This can be a benefit, as for Nicola Pagett, actress. 'I'm delighted the director is back in the control cubicle. All the responsibility is taken away from you.' Again, TV actors are used to this and the director's talkback into the studio from the gallery.

To sum up. To produce quick results, the director needs a speedy actor with a rhythm of work suited to radio, not an actor who is insecure or forced into taking the wrong short cuts. By the time the first successful take has gone into the can, a great deal has been decided. At the worst, the director could realize that the actor has been miscast. There is little or no time for an actor who is slowly getting there, or one who is floundering and might sink, or who is already below the water.

If you want a return booking!

Don't turn up late or walk in at the last minute. Don't open the script envelope at the studio door.

Don't wear rustling clothing with jangly jewellery.

Don't blame the retake on the other actors. (Never even comment on why there is a retake.)

Don't rush off to the next microphone as soon as your bit finishes in the scene.

Don't be a script rustler, a popper, a blaster, start scratching yourself, or go 'dead.' (See Chapter 4 for popping and blasting.)

Don't 'up-microphone' the other actors by 'giving them the eye-line', the 'grunts' and the 'umms', and by increasing your volume.

When you fluff, don't delay.

Don't panic from 4.00 p.m. onwards, when there's a complicated set-up and everybody is working against the clock.

Never try something new on the fifth retake.

And – horror of horrors! – never nag the director about rescheduling your part so you can get off earlier.

Hamish Wilson, director:
It's not like the army, but I expect my actors to be there ten or fifteen minutes early. Some actors make a lot of money in commercials, voice-overs, and when someone comes back after taking a lunch break of two hours for this because they've dashed off to another studio, it pisses me off. It's happened on two occasions in the last three years. The actors concerned have not repeated it, and they have been asked back... After a wretched day's rehearsal teaching, I have walked up to a student actor and said, "I'm sorry, you haven't done any work on it. Nobody told me, I heard it".'

Chapter 4

At the Microphone

Steve Nallon, actor and playwright:
At first the microphone frightened the life out of me. It was like meeting the TV camera for the first time. But what's a mike? It's only a black object two inches away from your nose.

Penny Gold, director:
Radio microphones are terrifyingly acute lie detectors. It's difficult for actors' performances of a general professional standard to get by them.

Liane Aukin, director:
I say to trainee students (though not to actors in the studio) that you cannot lie to the microphone – if the thought is not clear to the actor, the lines will not work. It is important you are clear on your intention on every line, that you understand it. You can get away with it in theatre in a way, but on radio you have to be very natural and very truthful. You've got to think it and feel it.

GET THE KNOWLEDGE

You could be faced with one microphone or a cluster of them. There are different types of microphone:

Mono single, or stereo pairs: on stands or boom.

Narrator's mike: usually set up with a table and chair, close screens around it, and a neutral acoustic.

A single lapel microphone: called the Lavalier, used for intimate thoughts and rapid movement, and sometimes outside-studio work (OB).

You usually stand to a stereo pair of microphones, the range of which is a semicircle.

Microphones have a *direction* and a *field*. If you step out of this, or extend your head out of it, you *go into the dead* (mono) and *out of phase* (stereo). You need to know where the *front* (mono) is and the *centre* (stereo). The Spot SM shows you where you should be and where you could go *off mike*.

Stereo has *left* and *right*. The director will tell you about this within the particular set. Some directors use stage left and stage right, and so the microphone represents the audience. With others, it is your own left and your own right. There is no one language for this, unfortunately, but it is over to the production team to get it clear. Mark it on your script.

In a group scene, the microphones are not set at a height for you alone. Ideally, the live end of the microphone should be level with your chin. The SM will set it (or the stereo pair) at the average height of the actors in the scene. You can direct your voice down to it, if you are higher. But be careful if you have to stretch and strain upwards to it. This is not an efficient stance for you as a performer and you can ask for the height to be changed. Sometimes you can be miked separately.

Take care that nothing comes between you and the microphone (or stereo pair). If you are crowded in for a scene, make sure nobody is blocking you. The professional convention is that people part and give way to you automatically for your cue, and when you have had your turn, you move back again. Do not let the script get between your mouth and the microphone.

Treat the microphone like the human ear. If you shout, move further away or turn off (stereo). If you whisper, move nearer. See page 48 for positions.

Popping and blasting

You have to beware of these two notorious dangers.

Popping: To *pop* is to sound a 'p' or a 'b' too close to the microphone and so distort the sound. The microphone relays this as a low-frequency thud, or popping sound. It can also happen with 'wh—' questions, like, 'Who?' and 'What?'

Blasting: To *blast* is to raise your volume suddenly and cause distortion.

Only through the cubicle speakers, will the director and his team hear you popping and blasting. This is a constant problem because, until you are told, you do not know in the studio that you have done it. You learn through common sense and experience to avoid it, just as in filming you know when you have 'hit your mark'.

Do not let out too great a force of air from your mouth, especially on the popping 'p' and 'b'.

Keep to a constant level and do not suddenly raise your volume without altering your position at the microphone.

Professional radio actors do not pop and blast once they have got their levels and they know their position in the sound set, but it is impossible to avoid it totally. You need to make the appropriate adjustment.

It becomes more of a problem when you move your position nearer the microphone, shifting from position three (conversation) to position one (interiorizing, intimate). Pop and blast are the terrible twins of radio, but there is lots more advice to follow, especially about acting at position 1, the closest to the microphone.

You have already been warned but it bears repeating: NEVER touch the microphone and NEVER blow into it.

Moving around the sound set: reality and illusion

Distance and travelling in the sound set are very different to the reality to be conveyed. It all depends on how the microphones and their fields are set up. You are blocked around the microphone in any of five positions and you move from one position to another. These switches are directed precisely and you must mark them down in your script. You can often make your own contribution in the detail to enrich your work. This chapter will help you to understand the paradox of travelling in a radio play scene. Getting from point A to point B in the scene does not necessarily mean you have to travel there; that being only one of the production options. Some times point B can come to you.

Both perspective and space are also different in the radio studio; they can expand and contract in ways forbidden to the film camera. Film must obey the physical laws of moving bodies in the visual field, although now flying and suchlike can be simulated by using computers. Similarly, in getting on and off and around the stage, you obey the laws of gravity and the physics of physical movement. The radio medium is totally liberated and you can apparently appear and disappear in any space, at any time, and be moved around the sound picture as fast as the listeners' ears can cope. Most radio plays represent real life and that imposes its own, easily-understood conventions. Radio allows the director to 'cheat', to fake some of this by speeding up or slowing down for emphasis, or by cutting out small portions which would otherwise impede the flow of the scene. 'Cheating' is well-known as a term on stage and in film. For example, on stage you often 'cheat' the process of eating by speeding it up and often by not putting food in your mouth. You will discover that some of your radio movements can be cheated, especially entering and leaving a room, and they need not follow the strict logic of life as it is lived. Realism in all plays is only a sort of selection and a branch of impressionism. There is an old folk warning that says, 'Believe half of what you see, half of what you read, and none of what you hear.'

Liane Aukin, director:
Think of the microphone as mostly like a camera lens, so the further off you stand, the more distant you are. It reflects the actual distance you travel. But it's not all like that, the microphone field is not logical, and distortion sets in. Ten feet away can sound like twenty feet away. You don't really know how far off you sound and you depend on the cubicle. It's an unrealistic distancing and it gives the director huge scope for illusion.

I will explain the five positions at the microphone and how each demands different techniques in voice and movement; and how you can apparently travel from A to B. You will notice that directors often describe movement on the model of an imaginary 'room', and 'entering the door', because many scenes are located in domestic rooms. This 'room' communicates spatial situations and solutions in a sort of shorthand and I find it most useful for teaching. It is easy to get this imaginary 'room', with its 'door' boundary, into your head and then to transpose spatial perspectives into other sorts of locations.

The five positions

Position 1. Closest to the microphone (interiorizing, intimate).
Position 2. Your mouth about half an arm's length away (intimate talk – secrets
Position 3. An arm-length away (conversation).
Position 4. *Moves* off, and halfway across the 'room'.
Position 5. *Moves* further away; at the 'door' of the room; and outside.

In each of these positions, you have to work out the placing of your feet (at the correct marks), how you can move your feet, your body from the waist (*turns*), and your *head focus* or *head concentration* (head moves). And then you get all those to work together for you in your position, without freezing into your stance.

Movement: *Switching* or *shifting* from position to position is one way to indicate movement, done most often. But you can travel across the sound picture by using the limits of the microphone. It depends on the microphone type and you do it by shifting slightly off to the dead side or by a turn away. It then sounds as if you have gone a distance though it need be no more than a head move and a step or two. I call this a *shift,* to differentiate it as a technique. Movement can be achieved by a combination of using positions and *shift.*

I have to give a little warning here. In this book, I have systematized microphone blocking as the 'five positions' and the *shift* and *switch,* although the terms are not known as such in BBC studios. Directors don't usually give notes about microphone placing in this specific detail. Rather, a director says to move closer by a step or a few inches. When I teach, I give notes such as, 'Could you try a shift there to microphone left?' or 'Shift from position 3 to position 1'.

This is the vital chapter about how you put your microphone skills to work: your blocking, your positions or placing, the shifts, switches and the microphone *focus* or *concentration* you need to achieve. You must put together all you have learnt so far. Think of the five basic positions as widening circles moving outwards from the microphone, and of the microphone as the same fixed point in their circumferences. It is important you think of these five circles as dynamic, as circles of energy, because you must not become frozen.

These dynamic uses of your position, and switching from one position to another as required, will come to you with experience. It is an exacting skill. When I outlined this chapter to director Hamish Wilson, he said, 'You must get over to training actors that they use the positions actively. I would regard these positions of yours as a sort of coarse tuning.' It is a crucial bit of advice from a professional and I have learnt a lot from him myself.

Hamish stresses that each of the positions should free up the actor's movement. 'When I teach acting students, I have to break this truth to them – *they can move.* I joke that some of their first attempts turn out like the gangster movies. Having got that correct distance from the microphone, say shoulder-to-wrist bone away, they get their feet stuck – mentally – in concrete. They have to break out of what I call "stand-and-deliver" acting. So I play group ring-a-ring-a-rosies to move them around the microphone field, and then we talk to the mike, and we say "Hello!". And yes, till students gain confidence, some stand there with their script, sweating, and with that look on their faces that says like William Tell's son, "Shoot, father, for I am unafraid"!'

Think with your head: *head moves* and *focus*

To summarize – each position is to be considered in relation to these three factors: feet marks, body turns, and head moves or head focus. The microphone is so sensitive that moving your head, either sideways or up-and-down especially, gives very different results. To put it into studio language – in each of these positions, the way you hold and use your head 'goes' differently to the microphone.

I have invented a special term for these head moves: *head focus* or *head concentration*. In other words, you have to think with your head when you are at the microphone, as well as your mouth, all the time. You use head focus, for the most part, to gain the effect of the body shifts.

Crucially, you should not look down when you speak. This is because of the way sound travels. The low frequencies reach the microphone if you look down and some of the high frequencies are lost as they travel forward to the floor. The result is that you sound downright muffled if your head is right down. If it is halfway down, you sound somewhat distant. Perhaps some more technical information is needed to explain this. High frequencies are crucial for making the words intelligible and they travel in a more directional manner than the low frequencies. With your head focus mistakenly dropped too low, the listener perceives fewer of the voice's high harmonics and they find your voice less present to their ears. You end up sounding dull. The director gets the impression that you are boring and you do not want to run that risk. The high frequencies make your voice interesting and uniquely characteristic of you, and they give that edge to your performance.

If you are tired you may occasionally let your head sink. But your professionalism should keep you on guard against this, because actors are trained to keep the head up. If it does happen, the SM or director should notice it fast. The danger is that you may tilt your head slightly down and this too will have an impoverishing effect on your performance. It causes a surprising loss of acting quality. When it is noticed, the note comes over the talkback, 'Were you looking down?' You will say 'No', of course. It has to be admitted that the actor concerned nearly always replies with a surprised 'No'. But everybody is then alerted to keep the head well up, in correct head focus.

There is one further trap for you at the bottom of the script page, and the page-turnover. Your head can fall, if you are not cautious, as you reach nearer the bottom of the page. This sounds very odd within the control cubicle. The actor's speech grows muffled and then suddenly un-muffled at the top of the next page, after the turnover. The contrast is worse if that particular speech is long. It sounds even more peculiar in narration or a short-story reading. It signals on broadcast to the listener that you are moving about and yet there is no reason within the context for you to do that. The solution is to keep your script well up, as well as your head, and to keep in mind your head focus all the time. Concentrate! Shorter actors have to keep their heads well up as the microphone is often set too high for them.

Check list: positions and moves

Switching from one microphone position to another is a *shift* (my term).

Feet *positions* are called *marks* (film term) and you have your *position*.

Make *turns* with your body, from the waist, when you keep your feet *to their mark*.

Concentrate on your *head moves*, your *head focus*.

Position 1: closest work

Position 1 is as close to the microphone as you can get, used especially for interiorizing (spoken thoughts). Position 1 is also used for intimate dialogue and asides. Again note that different actors' voices go to the microphone in different ways and a male voice with a lot of resonance and bass pitch, called bass tip-up, has to be placed a couple or more inches away. At least in this position, your script won't get in the way and the most individual aspects of your voice are on show.

Popping and blasting

Now we come to a full discussion of the terrible twins, popping and blasting, to which you are most exposed in position 1. Too near and you will distort, especially by *popping*. This is caused by a 'p' or a 'b', plosives, or anything similar, directed too closely into the microphone; actually a misdirected puff of breath that blows the microphone coil out of its mounting. It is immediately noticeable over the speakers (in the control cubicle) as a popping sound or thud, or something louder. The note will immediately come over the talkback, 'You're popping the mike'.

Hamish Wilson teaches students the dangers of popping firstly on an old-fashioned ribbon microphone, an STC. 'I get them to do *Peter Piper*. Sooner or later you get a couple of beauties, and I get them to listen to it on the recording. I explain that this pop, and it sounds more like a large naval gun going off, is caused by the wave at the base of the plosive. Then I give them the solution – to turn slightly off. I do *Peter Piper* almost standing at the microphone to show them, but that's done by breath control. It's not easy to pop on a Neumann microphone, but a 414 mike pops even if you wave a script near it. Popping does not happen often until you start working close. For an acting class, we have Collector's Pops of the Week. Some of the great names of radio do it because they are working at the edge of technology and of technique.'

Blasting is similar – a sudden increase in volume that distorts. Blasting has the same solution. A technically proficient actor is neither a popper nor a blaster. Again, you have to voice accurately and with subtlety, working from your position and head focus. You can notice for yourself a lot of popping in actuality and news interviews, where the ordinary public or politicians cannot be positioned accurately, or they move their position, and no retakes are possible. Technically, this should be kept to a minimum in radio actuality and it should never occur in radio plays (though you can spot it once in a blue moon).

You won't hear yourself popping or blasting because it can only be heard when it comes through the speakers in the control cubicle. But you will have been given your position when levels were set at the beginning of a sequence. You should be experienced enough to move your head if you raise volume, and to beware of the dangerous plosives, p's and b's, so you can use breath control and turn slightly off. Again, I must stress it is your responsibility not to blast or pop, so mark up your script where there is potential for the terrible twins. It is the film equivalent of losing your light.

In position 1, working across the microphone, you avoid popping and blasting

Working across the microphone

To get over the problem of popping and blasting, the director can give the note, to *work across the mike*. You work sideways to the microphone, as closely as possible with your cheek practically touching the live part. Your lips should be parallel with the front of the microphone if it is mono. If a stereo pair, you must stay at the same angle to the microphone as when you last spoke out loud. Otherwise, you will suddenly leap to another spot in the sound picture. (Of course, if this is intended, you will be blocked like this.) Your head focus here means that your lips do not move beyond the centre line. If you do, you will sound muffled.

The technical reason for working across the mike is that sounds and breath do not travel along the same path. Sideways on, your breath travels past and is no problem. The deeper notes in your voice travel in all directions, and in closer positions are picked up clearly by the microphone. The higher frequencies, to explain this again, travel in a narrow cone from your mouth. They are blocked by solid objects, like your head. So, if your head is not in focus, not only will your voice miss the microphone, but it will be masked as well. The director will tell you precisely how to move, from either a step or two back, to two or three inches.

Radio DJs often move forward into position 1 to give a sexier impression of themselves. It is one of their tricks of the trade, because it brings out the lower, more masculine tones, through bass tip-up. You may know of pop shields fitted on microphones. They are sponge covers, but give no protection in spite of their name. They can help with popping only in position 2 and with page turns which cause minor air disturbance. They give no protection against blowing into the microphone.

Position 2: intimate thoughts and *narrator's mike*

Position 2 is for intimate dialogue and conspiracy. It is also used for narrator's mike when you are the story-teller, or you talk to yourself, or sometimes to interiorize inner thoughts (though this is usually done at position 1). At position 2 you are about half an arm's length away from the microphone. This involves another aspect of technique, the final frontier in vocalizing.

Once you have got this close, and even more so in position 1, the microphone is able to pick up all of what is called your *vocal mechanism*. The listener will be able to hear smacking of lips, labial clicks, dryness of the lips, and particularities of your mouth such as the 'sss' and 'shhhs', involuntary whistling, and, yes, false teeth. These will be emphasized if your mouth is dry, so beware. Of course, part of the interest and pleasure for the listener in this close work is the intensity of voicing. But any structural problems with your vocal mechanism will be exposed in this position, just as the richness of what you have to offer can fully emerge. You learn to give more intensity and less volume, in a much more controlled way than film.

It is one of the great pleasures of radio listening to hear stars such as Anna Massey, Alan Rickman and Judi Dench in such intimacy, and any actor who has a worthwhile performance to give. Some stars of stage and television can fare less adequately at the microphone or give eccentrically interesting performances. Such was Jill Bennett, who was splendid in radio Noel Coward, but had three obvious faults in her vocal mechanism that went to the microphone all too easily.

If you are using narrator's mike, it is often within a set of its own. You could be sitting at a table, with headphones, and be surrounded by screens. The microphone is pointed at your forehead or your chin and this is for a good practical reason. Do not be put off. It is to minimize problems with your vocal mechanism, especially those

Position 3 (conversation) at the stereo pair microphone

lip smacks and teeth clicks. It can also deal with any problems caused by false teeth – as one studio manager put it to me, 'Let's face it, a surprising number of radio actors have false teeth and that is what we have to work around.' Another warned about wigs, especially nylon, which can cause a terrible noise on the microphones.

In positions 1 and 2, the listener concentrates totally on the speaking character, so any peculiarities must be ironed out. You have to know how your own voice goes to the microphone, in all five positions, and how to respond with technique if a problem arises.

Position 3: conversation scenes

Most radio scenes are ordinary conversation in domestic rooms. They usually require position 3, with your mouth about an arm's length away. That is the mark for your feet. You have to remember something technical here – when you raise the volume of your voice, you turn away, make a *turn*. Now you are this far away from the microphone, you must check your head focus and make sure your script does not block or muffle your voice between you and the microphone. I find when I am teaching students in position three, these are the notes I repeat most often.

Position 4: *moves* off and halfway to the 'door'

Picture for yourself all five positions within a domestic room, say a living room. Position 4 is halfway (plus) to the exit door, while position 5 is at the door itself and outside. We have just come from position 3, which is at the fireside or the sofa perhaps. It is a matter of directing style, of course. Some directors keep the action and sound picture bunched up close to what I call the sound centre; but others pan open the microphones more broadly and allow a bigger sound picture. You can hear this for yourself as you listen to a domestic scene where a character enters in the door. Do they suddenly 'leap' from the door to position 3? Or is there a middle ground they can inhabit (position 4)?

Of course there are many different sound pictures and sets. Often you are placed in position 4 to open out the picture a bit more and it could be that the action is set in a larger space, such as a factory, or hospital ward.

Position 5: *moves* further away

Position 5 gathers together all of your moves off, including exiting away from the scene, going behind a screen, up the stairs and into corners of the studio. Your biggest technical demand here is adjusting the level or volume of your voice as you move away and shift the relations of your head, and the line of your voice, to the microphone. Jane Morgan cites the example of actor Philip Voss who manages in all microphone positions 'to play it big without being an assault on the ears, big but not loud, because loud can sound ugly after a while.' On this same issue, Elizabeth Spriggs believes, 'You do not open the floodgates as much as on the stage, but you still use the same power, sending it down a tiny little channel. That makes it more tiring because you have to hold back a bit, but when you let it out on stage, it's a release. But it's just as emotional and often there are tears.'

Shifting from one microphone position to another

One of the greatest technical skills for a radio actor is to shift from one position to another, and to achieve correct focus each time. It may also be necessary to change from one microphone to another. The director could put the delivery of, for example, an intimate aside into another set but without stopping and restarting the sequence. So the actor has to move from position 3 in the first set into position 1 in the second set. Actor Matthew Morgan says, 'It's the trickiest thing to do. You change to an internalized style of performing for the "voice-in-the-mind". You have to divorce yourself suddenly from the scene you are playing.'

Hamish Wilson illustrates from his *Dracula* production, with Bernard Holley (as the character Jonathan Harker) whispering intimately at the moment of opening Dracula's coffin, and then finishing in a scream. 'It was extraordinarily difficult to do, and success was due to Bernard's technical handling of the microphone. He had taught himself about microphones because of his other production work. We went from close-up on him as he opened the coffin, to the scream. Bernard moved from close-up to away and his turn-off for the scream (from position 1 to 3 and turn). He used a combination, both his physical movement and control of his voice, so that the core of his voice went past rather than straight on to the microphone. The needles of the VUs did not go off the end stops. My studio manager did not have to use the compressor to the maximum, or "set the compressor to stun", as we say.

'Whereas, when I directed Kate Murphy in her first radio play, *Elephant Dances*, I spent twenty minutes explaining this and that to her, and got her to sit in the cubicle while I moved around the mikes and told her to listen to my voice changing. And she won the Sony Award for that play, for the best radio actress of the year. It was a tribute to the truth of her performance and not – primarily – to technical ability.'

Diana Bishop tells of the changeover from mono to stereo and the worry producers (as they were then called) had about positioning. 'In my first stereo production, producer Charles Lefeaux asked me over the talkback if I was standing on my right foot or my left foot! I couldn't believe it was all so incredibly crucial and I replied that I was equally divided between the two. Producers got easier after that, but at first there was great stress over exactly what your position was. My initial reaction to stereo was that if it was going to be so crucial, it was very difficult.' Positioning is still one of the director's main worries.

The microphone is everything

The demands of the five positions are the foundation for the studio. But production is not as mechanical and specific as this. The microphone is everything. It becomes: your listeners; the other characters you speak to; and when interiorizing, your 'me' inside speaking to the 'I' of your outer body. As Hamish Wilson says, 'Sometimes it is all of these things, even the room, and you have to bring students to an understanding of that relationship.' The five positions also depend on each individual set and how the microphones are panned open, and therefore on the extent and limits of their field. You can move off and out of the sound picture in three ways:

- Move off from position 4.
- Move slightly to the dead side of the microphone, especially if it is that sort of microphone (usually an older type).
- Turn away or 'oblique other character' as it is sometimes called.

Now you must understand perspective and movement in the radio scene, directing choices and paradoxes. This section gives you an insight into production as actor-director combined, and there are important rules to learn.

Getting from A to B: you must 'travel on the line'

There are a number of ways available to the radio director to get you from A to B in a scene – not only moving you there as in filming.

Shift physically: from one position to another in the dialogue. You enter the door, say, and keep moving (your approach) till you reach the other character – from position 5 to position 3 (conversation). Take this piece of script:

1. **FX (SPOT): DOOR VIOLENTLY OPENED.**

2. **FREDDIE:**   Hi, honey, I'm home! [shifting from position 5 to 3] Your worst nightmare. How restless, the creatures of the night.
[To position two still speaking]

3. **VICTIM:**   [breathing and whimpering in terror, position 2]

Panel operator fades you in and out: while you stay at the same mark. To make an approach, you are faded in. This is the paradox I mentioned earlier: B comes to you! But it does not sound as effective as when you shift. You do not get the opportunity to fully embody the lines because you make little or no physical movement. It suits ordinary approaches in standard production and can be the only viable choice in basic production, in a small studio.

The *head shift*: my term for this technique. You use your head mostly (head focus) to get into and out of the dead side of the microphone, and you do not need to step far, if at all. Here you are making the microphone field work for you. This demands precise head focus.

Change location: the director ends the scene at location A and restarts at location B. The story brings you to a certain point and then the next scene restarts at another location. To help you get this production point into your mind, think that the microphone 'does not follow you down the garden path'. For example:

1. MAUD:	[At location A] What about coming with me into the garden?
2. ALFRED:	I'm willing and waiting for you.
3. FX:	FADE OUT TO BLACK AND FADE IN NIGHT GARDEN ATMOS.
4. MAUD:	[Restarting at location B] Oh, horrible – bats!

Other 'travel' techniques: there are other choices available, such as opening several different microphones simultaneously, but I do not want to get bogged down here. Sometimes the script says WE GO WITH, and this technically means the getting from A to B is continuous. Two microphone pairs are set up and you walk from one field into the other while the panel operator crossfades. Alternatively, you might be miked with a Lavalier (on your lapel). But whatever the director's choice, production demands that:

WHEN MOVING FROM A TO B, YOU MUST ALWAYS 'TRAVEL ON THE LINE'.

It is an important rule to remember. As Liane Aukin, director, explains, 'There is no point in making any move unless you are speaking too. It's a rule actors new to radio must get into their minds because they make a mistake in following their stage actor's instinct – they make a move before speaking. Sometimes the script doesn't offer this opportunity and as director you need to give the actor a special line, so he can "travel on the line". As long as we, the listeners, hear the equivalent of a "Hi everybody!" line, we know he's arriving.'

Look at this mid-scene example. Jill is sitting and Jack is at the hotel bedroom door:

1. JILL: I'm waiting, darling, here on the bed.
[position 2]

2. JACK: Hold on, just get the key turned in the door – you never know. [position 5]

3. JILL: A boy's gotta do—

4. JACK: Done! Here I am, ready or not!
[shifting to position 3, he 'travels on the line']

5. JILL: My lover boy—

6. JACK: Geronimo! [shifting to position 2]

Elizabeth Spriggs comments on the change from the previous days of mono, 'Today the equipment does so much more for you. Technique has changed in moving in and out. The danger is that of being less interpretative. Young actors coming up know the equipment and less of the interpretation.'

Turn

Directors often call for a turn when the script requires you to shout or to express heightened emotion. The turn is made by bending the torso around from the waist, not stiffly, and moving your head to the side while keeping to your position. This technique keeps your voice level within an acceptable limit for the cubicle and yet allows you to vocalize expressively and with force. Your director will say, 'You'll need a turn for that shouting there'. Sometimes you bend around as far as you can and shout into the curtains or screens. You make sure you do not go into the dead (mono) or out of phase (stereo). Once you have learnt the turn technique it is up to you to realize when it is needed and to use it without the director's prompting, so be sure to note it on your script. You can move your feet, and as Hamish Wilson says, 'Mobility in front of the microphone is important, for energy and space.'

There are smaller movements of head, body and arm which help to 'colour', as it is termed, your dialogue. They bring your radio body language into use, adding liveliness and presence. Rearrange your torso and head position occasionally, in relation to the microphone, though being careful not to move your feet away from their position. Try veering your head a bit to the side, only by twenty degrees, and then back, but without your voice level going down. (If you think of the axis of the microphone as noon on the clock, you can move your head around to two o'clock.) You may want to raise your volume a little as you move away. Just altering the relation of your mouth to the axis of the microphone is enough in a stretch of dialogue to give variation. That is adding colour by torso and head. Finally, you can make an arm movement or some sort of gesture with your free arm. Your free arm is often needed in the studio and can send a small or large wave of energy through the line. Your director will say, 'Give it a bit of colour there, it's getting lifeless and talking-heads.' Clothing may rustle effectively, or in a classic play, it could be Spot period dress. Of course this 'embodying' can be overdone, and clutter and weigh down the words.

For Hamish Wilson, director in BBC Scotland, 'Radio is as physical as any other form of speaking. I was an actor for seventeen years before I became a radio play director and I speak from that experience. The actor must use body and movement to enhance and define character within the audio image.' He notes that 'more than a 45° turn needs a movement of the head back to the mike. Turning adds to intimacy and naturalism.'

He gives the illustration of an actor in *Canticle to Leibowitz* getting on a horse. 'I heard him get on that horse, I heard everything in appropriate sequence, the foot on the stirrup, and the up into the saddle.' The actor there had thought through the detail and logic of a complex movement. Actress Anna Gilbert says, 'I have to do everything to give the sense of lived experience, for the listeners to get the impression that they are getting lives lived, rather than a shadowy radio world. It's to stop the muffling that radio seems to impose, to stop seeming contrived. It is so easy to forget all you are doing, to lose detail and sharpness.'

Your relationship with the microphone

Play to the microphone – 'play the mike'.

Keep within the microphone field, also called the sound sphere.

Keep to your position, also called your blocking or mark.

Don't look at your scene partners, only glance.

Don't 'mask' your voice by getting something between you and the microphone.

'See' the microphone as a human ear and your favourite listener, and the other characters.

At the centre of the actor's technique is the microphone, a sort of sound telescope. It explores and exposes your vocal technique, cruelly

Figure of eight microphone enabling actors to face each other

sometimes, and relentlessly always. A wrongly stressed syllable or a mispronounced syllable is instantly noticeable. Worse, is a delivery that is not true to the character's feelings.

Playing to the microphone, 'playing the mike', is an absolute because you can rarely face the other actors directly. Blocking for a group scene is often in a semi-circle around the field of the microphone, typically a stereo pair. This field is called the sound sphere. Usually, you find yourself side-by-side with your scene partners and not face-to-face. Sometimes you cannot see your co-actors at all. They could be at another microphone, perhaps in a different acoustic and set, if that is what the script requires. You might all have to be 'miked separately', that is, placed at individual microphones. Your partners could be behind a screen or behind you. An alternative is that your scene partners step forward into and back out of the microphone field as their cues require. An exception is the 'figure-of-eight' microphone, the field of which is exactly that of its name. That sort of microphone enables you to face each other with the microphone between you.

Think of a two-hander scene, intimate and intense, that requires the maximum of communication between you. Although you play to the same microphone, you cannot use eye-contact with each other, but you can give glances, especially when innuendo is in the script. You certainly do not touch one another, unless requested to do so. Carole Boyd, who plays Linda Snell in *The Archers* summarizes, 'Stereo denies you that real contact because the sound sphere is so crucial and delicate. It's a bit dangerous to make eye contact and you could just get lost.' Yet you have to bring the microphone into the relationship, so that it becomes a three-cornered conversation.

Establishing eye-contact could make other actors uncomfortable and even distract them. It is reckoned to be bad technique. Having said that, you can give glances to 'keep in' and that is fine and welcome. You transmit energy back and forth and it is good for cueing. Just remember you need to keep your concentration on the script and if your eyes readjust their lens' focus to further off, you need that short time to refocus on the script in front of you. You might slip up. Don't be put off if the other actors do not glance much at you – they are being professional. Actor Kerry Shale explains how he does it. 'Almost always I "play the mike". Directors say, "Kerry, don't look at the other actors, - play the mike". So I imagine the microphone is the other character I'm acting with, or it's the listener. You use your instinct and I found my instinctive feeling is for how the voice is absorbed by the microphone.'

Pam Brighton though, director in BBC Belfast, prefers actors to watch each other and 'it is important that eyes and faces make connections – touching and holding too, I make it possible that they happen. They are acting and somewhere there's a mike hearing it. I just started using hand-held mikes, held by technicians following round the actors and moving with them, standing up and lying down, only from about a year ago. It works so well in intimate bed scenes, for example, and in movement scenes.'

Another way actors keep in is to gesture a lot with their free hand. A lot of waving goes on in the studio, sometimes wildly. This keeps you communicating with your scene partners, strange as it might appear. It is all part of our human signalling system in talk. Also it lets you energize more and underline what you say. It helps your breathing mechanism, keeps your body in play and relaxed, and your voice oiled. You can even use arm waving to underplay, so that you hold back the forcefulness of the words to get their subtlety, but let out the energy through your arm and hand. Try it and see. And keep waving to vary delivery and break it up. You also get used to differing waves as some actors shake their hand up and down with every few sentences.

You must keep your focus on the microphone, otherwise you will 'mask' your voice – that is, your voice will not go as directed to the microphone. Accidentally holding your script in between your mouth and the mike is a common blunder if you are inexperienced. The simple rule for beginners is always to keep the microphone in your line of vision and not let the script get in the way. A moment's inattention, tiredness, and you lose what I call your 'head focus' or 'head concentration'. I do not apologize for insisting yet again, keep your script up and a bit to the side.

You must discover your own relationship with the microphone. For some that means imagining the microphone is a film camera but I will develop that a little later. In early training, it is best to imagine the microphone as a human ear. (See page 16.) Often actors 'see' the microphone as a single favourite listener. That transforms it into a receptive friend. Always remember that out there is someone you are talking to and the microphone is your vital link. The listeners are not one big audience, but are individuals, and each one wants to hear you. That especially holds if you are alone in the studio with a monologue or a story reading. Keep this in mind, and you will be on your way to sounding intimate, subtle and naturalistic, when you need to, and you will communicate your character.

The microphone has a magnifying effect, though it is not similar to the magnifying effect of the actor in the stage space. The differences for radio are twofold: scale and perspective. You often need to underplay and be more subtle, and you rarely use the projection needed for stage, unless that is in the style of the production. So as regards scale, you 'bring down' your voice and your performance, and you do not use the energy and 'throw' of the stage voice. Perspective is how voices are placed into the sound picture in scale and in relation to each other. It is how near and far you sound away from the listener. The microphone alters perspective, and magnifies intimacy and subtlety. You must not, literally, put a foot or your head wrong.

To summarize, the microphone becomes for you the other characters and your audience, your friend and your single line of communication. The direction of your voice (or 'voice-line') has to replace the eye-focus or 'eyeline' technique you use on stage and film.

PUTTING YOU IN THE SOUND PICTURE

Acoustics are what make one location sound different from another, such as a living room, a street or a factory. The SMs build sets inside the studio by drawing curtains, setting up screens and moving carpets, to try to simulate the acoustics of different environments. More from the FXs on CDs and cassette, may need to be layered on top of the studio output as it gets into the cubicle. For the cathedral acoustic, for example, the cubicle provides what could be called the aural 'scenery' and may feed it through the computer synthesizer.

Studio sets use the minimum of furniture, chairs, tables and doors. Also, BBC studios have high ceilings, some 13 feet, so sound leaks all over the place. Take a modern bedroom in a council house, which in real life has a mixture of surfaces (windows, mirrors, wardrobe) that reflect the sound back and soft furnishings (bed, comfortable chair) absorbing it. Such a BBC bedroom set will emphasize the soft aspects of sound and not be as echoless as the real thing. The rule here is to get a definition the listener can recognize.

Or take a wood-panelled Jacobean room, or a jogging scene out on the moors. You can achieve these scenes by location recording, and that is the more natural and now often the less expensive option, or by the computer processor – the BBC's digital systems such as Sadie and Audiofile – which works miracles. Some systems, such as Quantac in Broadcasting House, have all sorts of acoustics stored within. If you record in a swimming pool, the result is qualitatively different from a studio production, because echoey sounds and voices are altered by the water surface, the large hall and the water vapour in the air.

Scenes located outside in the open air are hardest of all to achieve convincingly in a studio that does not have the computer system. On a moor, a hill, a street, the edge of a forest, or on top of a castle, voices are 'dead' in that there are no reverberating echoes into space. Also they can pick up unexpected echoes from trees, buildings, the castle walls. There are many subtleties in the real-life mix and film recording can play most convincingly with them. But radio play broadcasting is not up to these reverberating patterns and their complications. The radio solution is to place most of these scenes in the dead room, to give them as little reverberation as possible, and to mix the atmos on top. This is fine for the seashore, a field, and the moors, but less satisfactory for scenery which is more of a mix. It is also possible to make the voices echo, with the 'echo mike' or by synthesizer.

So, the 'outside' set is deadened as much as possible, though the floor might be bared to the concrete. The unfortunate result of this is that the 'outside' set is nearly always too small for the action that is supposed to be taking place there, and does not allow much in the way of moves (positions 4 and 5). The largest dead rooms available in the BBC or in external facility houses are not that large. One panel SM in the World Service confessed to me, 'with open-air scenes you really can't win unless you have Audiofile to load an atmos on top.'

Another problem is the notorious ticking clock. Nearly always it must be mixed on to the dialogue in post-production, and not as a Spot clock, for the good reason that cutting and matching takes would otherwise be impossible. The ticks would not match up regularly. So the actor does not hear the clock, but in the broadcast scene the ticks give a background pulse to the pace of the dialogue. The director must give the actors the rhythm of the scene.

As you listen to a variety of acoustics across many plays, you realize the director's choices have their limits. What acoustics read effectively? I call this production choice the *If I'm Driving It Must Be Raining* Rule. Often it is not enough to indicate the car acoustic by traffic background and changing gears during an average-size scene, as these can fade in significance from the listener's notice. Adding a further acoustic detail, the regular to-and-fro of the wind-screen wipers, gives an effective texture to the scene and can help build tension. Hence all that driving in the rain on the radio. But whatever the set and the acoustic, much of the acoustic is created by the actor's voice. Many directors have stressed this to me, pointing out that '70% of the acoustic is in the acting'.

Key questions

There are often queries about the details and construction of the sound picture. Knowing 'who; what; where; and how?' is essential for every actor's preparation. But production in the cubicle can sometimes be confusing. What appears to be the 'logic' of the sound set, with 'left' and 'right', can change within a scene. You can be 'moved' to another part of the sound picture by your microphone being switched over, and this all happens in the cubicle and on the control panel. You do not physically move. The director simply says, 'Don't worry, we'll switch you over there in the cubicle', or 'by magic over there'.

Blocking and directing styles:
the up-front set or the opened-out

Directors adopt either a more *up-front* style at the microphone with-in a narrow blocking field (position 3, conversation, rather than using position 4); or they allow the actors to roam more widely, in a larger sound picture (making more use of positions 4 and 5).

Penny Gold, director:
I don't mind the actors moving off the mike and I allow them almost as much movement as on stage. Other directors lament the loss of mono and insist on strict placings for their actors. Old-style directors are frightened of their actors moving off.

In the main, directors have two different styles in moving actors round the microphone field. Some keep the actors close and block them precisely. For the listener's sound pictures, in all those scenes in rooms, cars and streets, the characters are in close-up for the most part. This style is more *up-front*. In the basic production stu-dio (see page 00), there is no other choice, as wider moves are not physically possible in the space. Bringing nearly everything so close (mostly positions 1, 2 and 3) to the microphone in this way results in a sameness.

Other directors open out the sound picture more widely, and give the sense of a sound 'frame' about 15 feet wide and more. In listen-ing professionally, you should be able to detect this for yourself, as it gives the actors more space for embodying and it can come over more convincingly. In classic and genre acting (stage plays, thrillers, novels etc.), the director must open up the set, sometimes to the equivalent of a stage set, and that is what is in the 'mindscreen' of the listeners.

You have to pick up now on the subtleties of directing style. For example, Pam Brighton says, 'I try to get the actors to forget the microphones as much as possible. I set up two microphones and give the actors room to play it as physically as possible – so I drive the sound people crazy! I hate the old sense of actors standing around at the mikes.' Similarly, director Alan Drury, previously part-time in the BBC and now working as an independent, describes his use of a domestic set (the 'room'): 'I used to be fussy about where the actors were to be placed. But I find it much more naturalistic now to get the feeling of people in a room. I let them wander around, as if in a room, to get the feeling of that and then make sure that the microphones pick them up.' Liane Aukin com-ments, 'I personally don't worry how far away I'll place the actors till I get into the studio. If there is a door in the room, I prefer to place it at a slight angle to the left or the right. That's unless it has the dramatic function of being in the middle. Take John Whiting's first play, which we blocked like the stage play (it was written for the stage), with the sound substitutes for sofa and chairs, the door in the middle, and the microphone as the audience.' Actress Angela Pleasence expresses the fuller benefits of the 'opened-out' style: 'In radio, you can't minimize it, radio's emotions are very similar to theatre – it's not a minimalist form of creativity. It has to be large. I can't be doing with actors who have little previous radio experience, and who speak low and introspectively. I've worked with Gielgud on radio Shakespeare and his performance has no compromising – he goes the whole way as if the audience is there.'

The microphone as film camera

Hilary Norrish, director:
I always describe movements and the microphone as film shots. I say, 'Pull away', 'Follow'. I use shifting focus.

Liane Aukin, director:
Like the film camera, the microphone can pick up the expression in the eyes – it's up to the actor.

Some directors use the microphone as if it were a film camera. This can be exciting as a technique, especially in moves, in using portable microphones and Lavaliers, and in location work. This is the other stylistic tendency of radio drama – if it is not the 'stage-type', then it can be 'filmic', importing aspects of film's visual track. Liane Aukin finds it improves communication with the actors. 'It's the quickest way of making everybody see in their mind's eye the same thing. I talk of the close shot, the middle, with the camera fixed, of course.'

An actor can image the microphone as a film camera, though there are limits to this. It can be useful for memorizing perspective and for positions, and even for marking up your script. Liane Aukin continues, 'The actor can choose at times to give his own close-up by leaning in to the mike, if he is imaginative and responds to the script. The "film-microphone" idea helps him to work with others.' What is referred to here is a short shift from position 3 to 2, and back again, to give colour to the lines.

But the microphone is not a 'radio camera' in other respects. We say the film camera 'has a love affair' with such and such a star, but we do not talk of the microphone in the same way. It does not focus and select, rather it exposes everything in its field. It is not always helpful to image the field as the camera frame because it does not create the same perspective.

To return to Liane Aukin's point about using camera terms in notes: 'I like a cast when possible to know what's going on. So I say "I want to cut to a close-up", or "a long shot". On the script, the technical direction will say "on mike" and that means a close-up, like a head-shot. The moment I say that, I know the actor knows it. But it's not useful at other times. Personally, I think of it in terms of how do I get the picture. And it's also useful if I set up a second microphone because you set up second and more cameras all the time in film. There I'm thinking of cross-cutting, say from the dining table to the window-seat, it gives me the perspective and the background.' David Hitchinson also gives notes such as, 'a close one-shot' and 'a distant two-shot', and 'I'm coming in close to you on this'.

Actors at the microphone

Graham Padden
I find working in stereo more physical and natural, you're closer to the mike. I'm fascinated to see actors still talking to the mike rather than each other. It still does happen. You use your imagination to find your character's 'space' and this naturalness helps. But approaches and retreats are exaggerated because a short step makes much more difference in stereo, at the edge of the microphone field. That seems unnatural when seen in operation.

Matthew Morgan
In rehearsal, I use eye contact to get the rhythm, but not in the take. I fix the emotion in the mind and then fix it on the microphone. I have a habit of throwing up my left hand to get the energy for cues, my right is holding the script, of course. When Clive Brill directed me in the *Humphry Clinker* adaptation, he'd say, 'You have to drive this scene'. Right before the take, I would take a push against the wall for thirty seconds and on cue, I'd push off the wall and be straight into the scene. I felt different from the other actors, it gave my character an extra barrier, which was just right.

Steve Nallon
Actors don't like people watching them when they perform for radio. With comedy though, it's useful to have eye contact with the other actors which makes it slightly more dangerous.

James Aubrey
I'm a very physical actor, on stage too. Catch a good director and you can have him set up two microphones, so that when you heave over and roll on the floor, it's all recorded. You can be so alone and private, in a monologue, say, surrounded by metal screens at the end of a studio, it's so personal. You wouldn't even get that intimacy and electricity in a small studio theatre.

Kerry Shale
My arms used to flail around like a mad thing. And I used to shake, and bounce up and down on my knees a bit. That was nerves. Now, I try to keep my knees slightly bent, so they don't tense up, I'm more relaxed with the more radio I've done. When I approach a heavy emotional scene, I hang down and let my body raise up. Your voice will tense up if you're not relaxed.

Angela Pleasence
It's a microphone for God's sake! At the beginning I was scared but now I love it.

David Hitchinsin, director
It's like not having the microphone there. You have to relate to it as a person, or as the audience or another character, or like a film camera. Make it a tension diffuser.

Actors in studio sets

Kerry Shale
I enjoy yelling into screens in the corner and those weird convoluted dances around the studio. Overall, it's pretty simple, it's like finding your marks in a film, or like getting into film dubbing, it's a very particular talent.

Matthew Morgan
I'm not bothered by screens. I find some dead rooms are more effective than others. In *Maida Vale 7*, for a scene in a canvas tent, we lay down, hunched up, and that does all the work for you. The body reacts as it should.

Turan Ali, director
Sound is so subjective that you can organize a set that 'looks' all wrong. You can only go by what it sounds like in the control cubicle.

At times as a director you feel like closing the control cubicle curtains and getting on with it!

Working on location

Graham Padden, actor

There's an increasing tendency to do more on location. But what you can do as 'natural' is totally up to the technicians. We were recording *A Most Desirable Property* in a cul-de-sac with director Vanessa Whitburn and I had to do the vital dialogue – 'there's a tile off the roof' – with my back to the very house the plot was about! The technicians needed that blocking for the stereo picture. And all the neighbours came out to garden, pushed their lawnmowers about, and the techies had to be dispatched to bribe them back inside. *Golden Girls* is infamous in Pebble Mill. An actor pulled a ligament running and here was a sort of first – a case of someone injured on radio.

Christian Rodska, actor

The difference with location working is that it is justified if you have to run down a long road or over fells, for example, and if such movement is sustained through the whole play. However, there is so much you can do in the studio. And what it finally comes down to is, does the listener know it is on location? Is the product as good?

I've done it quite a lot, with Shaun McLoughlin, for example. We did a play in a swimming pool and had to protect the microphone with a condom. We did some Australian plays in a lake near Bristol. I've done jogging plays and mountain running, with director Kay Patrick. As an actor, you get signals from the environment. But the downside is that the script pages get wet from the rain, the wind makes the pages blow and become noisy. And say you are dragging a boat to shore with one hand and holding on to your script with the other, it puts other burdens on you.

Moir Leslie, actress

I've recorded in a convent school and in the confessional, where it was claustrophic and a tight scene – you didn't need imagination, as it was all there.

Jilly Bond, actress

In recording Ibsen's *A Doll's House* in a house in Kentish Town, we had more time allowed to talk together about the script. The first time I walked into a room in a scene, I felt an enormous atmosphere.

Tessa Worsley, actress

I've worked in boats in a Bristol reservoir and in a Hertfordshire field, and I have to be honest and say it helped with the idea of open space, but in terms of emotional feeling, it was dissipated. I missed the intense microphone work of the studio.

Pam Brighton, director in Belfast

It works if the scene is contemporary and outside. Actors respond well, climbing mountains, as in *Shout a Secret to the Stone*, with four Irish-Americans climbing the Mayo mountains, and *Seaside*, two women on a beach, swimming out and back, and we recorded in the middle of the night, it was wonderful. I am in production at weekends, and so office scenes are recorded in the BBC offices along with the toilets, which are mostly empty, and there's a corridor here which has been in every prison play I've done!

Jane Morgan, director

As one of the perpetrators of location work, I live to rue the day! It's useful on occasions, if it involves local people. I refute the idea that actors find locations better because the scenery can get in the way and the scenery may not be better.

Jeremy Mortimer, director

I work outside with a portable DAT [digital recording] machine, with an on-the-hoof, on-the-fly feeling. Actors and people around are not certain when you are recording. With the cast in a Balti Curry House, for example, as the waiter came along, an actor ordered and we caught it all. The actor says, Let's go for it now. The portability gives a real frisson to the day, around the streets or in the gents. It's possible to record in the lunch hour as well. OB [outside broadcast] recording is now cheaper and partly driven by cost, which may not be the best reason. I find it takes out the gap between director and actors, as the studio glass panel has gone. I can guide the actor by gesture and facial expressions, and I can travel and move the action more, panning shots so as to speak, and walking through buildings. When I recorded *Five Kinds of Silence*, a harrowing play with Tom Courtenay, we were all in a flat for three days, a cohesive experience. I never got away to hide behind the glass and Julia Ford's raw emotion was quite ovepowering, I couldn't talk for ten minutes.

Chapter 5

Lift it off the Page

BBC Radio Drama Company professional quip: *There are only four rules – speak louder, speak softer, go nearer the microphone, move further away.*

CREATIVITY AND CHOICES

Radio acting requires:
Subtlety: you often underplay, rarely overplay.

Exactness: of timing and positioning. You have to be ready and flexible.

Accuracy: of voicing, dialect and pronunciation and sense of style.

Speed and commitment: it demands more of you.

The skill is *Lifting it off the page*

Your task is not to read but to communicate – be spontaneous and fresh.
You have to do it almost as if the script wasn't there.
Beware of verbal fluffs (slips) – keep up your concentration.
Be a skilled sight-reader and coordinate your eye-mind-mouth-ear.

Radio acting is performing with the script held in your hand. This skill of acting while reading from a script is called 'lifting it off the page'. The actor's mental process goes from page-to-mind and from voice-to-microphone, yet it is still a memory task in some vital ways. But unlike other media, radio actors do not lay down the book.

First-time radio actors can find it a hurdle to perform with the script in hand, especially if they are accustomed to stage work. This is partly because of what laying the book down in stage rehearsal means. It is such an advance in building the role – a gaining of independence and physical release into more confident movement. There are also unwelcome associations from 'book in hand' productions on stage: public readings of new plays, 'walking through it', or filling in for an indisposed actor. All of these suggest incomplete performance. Some actors, however, experience how the script-in-hand performance can liberate their acting energies. As a radio actor, you build and create through a crucially different process while you retain your script as concrete support all the way through.

Your main anxiety about script-holding is to ensure the pages do not rustle, not even in the slightest. The most successful take may have to be abandoned if the director announces over the talkback into the studio, 'Sorry, stop. I heard a script rustle there'. The causes for the actor? Nervousness, inattention, accident or lack of experience. Be careful also not to tap on your script from boredom or for emphasis.

Holding a script, the radio actor cannot dry or forget his words during a take, at least not directly due to a memory lapse. That in itself should give you confidence, being free of one of the main causes of stage-fright. There is no prompter in radio drama. You have the advantage of being able to give all your concentration to the lines, undistracted by the demands of totally memorizing. Memory is at work, of course, in the detail of your performance. You need to be literally and mentally in touch with the words and see the whole play.

If a radio performer is unconvincing, the listener gets the impression that speech is merely being read and that the actors are mere 'talking heads'. Their alternating dialogue becomes an unreal game of ping-pong. Actor Andrew Sachs said that the best note he ever got from a radio director was from John Gibson in the 1960s: 'I want these words lifted off the page.' That is something that every director has to say. The actor's task is not to read but to communicate.

About creating the sense of dialogue, Jonathan James-Moore, Head of BBC Light Entertainments explains, 'The actor has to develop internal relations in the dialogue, rather than one person speaking and then another person speaking. It's difficult to direct these internal relations.' There is a complex process of memory involved in 'lifting', in the momentary shift of eye. It is from page to microphone, and the chain is really from the eye, leading ahead slightly, to mind and to mouth, and then monitored by the ear. It is a continuous, almost simultaneous loop of eye-mind-mouth-ear.

Fluffs (slips of the tongue) and spoonerisms can ambush all too easily, no matter how energized the actor is. Everybody's professional experience, however, is that the radio drama studio is a place of total concentration where corpsing is rare. As opposed to reading a speech in public, the eyes remain focused nearly all the time on the radio script.

This is not acting without risk, it is still all performance. Also it is within the rigid time budget of studio production, which brings its own dangers. But the radio actor has that clear autonomous aim from the beginning of production and is less cluttered. No wonder actors love radio work. Even Nicholas Craig, the comic actor-monster created by Nigel Planer in *I, An Actor*, begs greedily for more within his hectic schedule. 'And of course, one can do it on a Sunday which would be absolutely ideal for me.'

In radio auditions, you are tested for lifting it off the page and sight-reading. Director Ned Chaillet says, 'Actors are tested by their speed at picking up cues. They've got to remember they're not reading.' As Norman Painting, character Phil Archer and scripter of *The Archers* summarized: 'You have to do it almost as if the script wasn't there'.

Steve Nallon is revealing about his own 'page-to-mouth' process. 'To make it sound real, to make it natural, you have to "forget" what you've just read in the script. Then you have to say it as if it is fresh – and this process of "forgetting" is dangerous. You put it into your mind as if you had just thought of it. It's more natural for the actor, but it tends to make you more fluffy. If the director can understand you, then that is a great working process. But if you just read it, it will be correct, and boring. The "forgetting" is how the mind works, as it immediately tries to forget what you've read and say it as if fresh. I make it seem as if I had just thought of it. But the problem is that you are prey to mistakes – in one in eight sentences, you come up with a synonym, a word like the original in meaning. In sum, you have the script right in front of you and you try not to work "from" a script.'

Graham Paddock believes 'you've got to discover what you're reading on the page. It requires a lightness of touch in your playing. The difficulty for me is the *business* of being *spontaneous* with what I'm reading – that's the contradiction. It's between those two things.' Your rule, as with all acting, is: be spontaneous, be fresh.

Speed and commitment

Trust to instinct and technique for speedy production.

Production usually breaks up the scenes and storyline.

The play's 'hook' – the first thirty seconds – has to grab the listeners.

Radio production is speedy, terrifyingly so for the beginner. Once the first take is in the can, the actor is committed. As Christian Rodska puts it, 'You give a performance that is almost instant. I once did weekly rep, which must have something to do with how I work. Once you've recorded something, that's it, you can't go back.' Director Pam Brighton says, 'You have to do the impossible in a short time and what you are working off is an actor's instinct.'

One day in the BBC studio equals half-an-hour of broadcast time. The Radio 4 afternoon Thirty-minute Play is one day's production and the Monday Play is three. The grandest-scale production, such as Kenneth Branagh's *Hamlet* took five days. A long continuous production, for example, David Hitchinson's adaptation of the Bulgakov novel, *The Master and Margharita* in five one-hour episodes, took eight days.

It was even speedier in the old days of mono, up to the sixties, when plays were broadcast live. Sian Phillips recalls her first work in Cardiff, 'Radio drama producers were buccaneering types with a touch of the Red Queen. Lorraine Davies, the only woman producer in BBC Wales, had the temperament of a Cecil B De Mille. The control panel could just stand up to the thump of her fists as she lashed the maximum out of us. Radio is a maximum-effort medium!'

The 10.00 a.m. call to a radio drama studio suite starts usually with a read-through, director's notes, then a rehearsal in the first studio set. The first takes could be in the can before lunch, especially in a one-day schedule, or in the first part of the afternoon. Already the actor is committed to his or her character and performance. Contrast the stage actor's voyage of discovery through two, three or more weeks of rehearsal, and how stage actors hide or have not yet discovered their performances in their first read-through.

Directors usually expect you to come up with a performance at the read-through (see Chapter 3). John Taylor, previously director in Radio 5 drama, uses actor Paul Scofield as an example. 'He tries a line and tries it again. He'll keep finding his way with that line from the read-through on. He goes further and further into it. You can see each actor's process on from the read-through.' This production schedule leaves little time for what happens alongside in stage rehearsal: hypothesis-testing, theorizing, wider creative interpretation. You have probably found there is another item in this stage agenda, that is not openly declared. Actors find status rewards in rehearsal discussion and some can extend it for that reason. Just accept that however personally gainful and entertaining it is to chat, you have to keep most of it for the breaks. Careless talk might just cost you your next part.

Hilary Norrish, who has moved as director from BBC World Service to BBC Radio, credits actors' courage. 'You are asking them to lay down, in the afternoon of the first day, what takes weeks of stage rehearsal. It's instinct. In stage rehearsal, after all that preliminary bedding, actors usually return to their first instincts. There is no time to help the actors, you can feel terribly impotent as a director, every time I'm amazed at their courage.' Nicola Pagett explains from the actor's side, 'In theatre, the part becomes more yours in stages. You've got to trust in radio. There is no time for an argument, otherwise it'd be six o'clock before you started! The one enormous problem is to be very good in the time.'

Note that the opening of the play may not come first in the production schedule. Hence you may find useful the techniques for preparation, 'keeping in' as it is called, and concentration in Chapter 7. Disjointed production means that you have to know where you are. But the radio play's opening demands great care from the director, perhaps that bit extra than on stage or film. There is a production rule here. The first thirty seconds or so of a radio play must provide an interesting 'hook' to keep listeners engaged and away from their 'off' switch. Added to this is a signal sent to the listeners, that the play protagonist almost always speaks the first lines and establishes himself or herself from the top. This character's 'entrance' demands a lot of the actor. And it just might be the first sequence recorded, before the actor has much of that character tested for himself. The fact is, a radio play has to 'download' a lot of itself into its opening minutes of broadcast, and the director and the writer cannot afford to throw that 'hook' away.

This poses a special challenge to the actor playing the lead. Almost all plays written originally for radio, 'radio originations' as they are called, are dominated by a single, sympathetic protagonist, who is liable to be in most of the scenes and whose viewpoint dominates them. So in this respect a radio cast is more likely to be built around a main actor. The play usually has a storyline 'point-of-view' through this protagonist. Scripts which are adaptations from stage plays and novels can be more evenly distributed, have a variety of roles, and demand more ensemble acting with larger-cast scenes. However, scenes with more than four characters are difficult to real-ize in radio production. You will find that crowd scenes pose special problems for the director.

Radio originations mostly have two-hander and three-hander scenes. These are often on the pattern of two talking and then the arrival of a third, making a 2 + 1 scene, and sometimes a 2 + 2. I always refer to *The Archers* to illustrate technique, because it can stay by traditional radio conventions going back to mono. You will find most of the scenes in an episode which are not two-handers are 2 + 1, or 2 + 2. So the radio actor, especially of BBC afternoon plays, is usually faced with tighter dialogue in the script with fewer characters to relate to and with less complex scenes, than in film and mainstream theatre.

Working to the microphone and your 'first audience'

Cubicle and studio are your 'first audience'.
You may feel isolated.

The radio actor is relatively isolated. True, he or she is in the studio with the other actors and Spot. But for takes, the director must be seated at the control panel in the control cubicle. In the days of mono, the curtain across the window from the control cubicle into the studio was drawn across. The radio producer really did fly blind then so as to concentrate on what came through from the studio microphones. So how do you get feedback? What benefits come from your 'first audience', that is everybody in the drama suite, and will you find the sort of feedback you get in stage rehearsal and performance?

The greatest contrast is with acting on the stage, with presence. The stage magnifies its actors and the audience focuses on them, it is a higher level of intensity in playing, energy and projection. In the run of performances, the actor responds to his different audiences, night by night. While in the film studio, the actor gives his perfor-mance to the camera but also benefits from the 'first audience' of those crowded on the set. The actor enjoys a secondary presence live in the film studio, although like radio, it is an indirect medium. In the radio studio, you barely find a 'first audience' among fellow actors, director and Spot, and you have the least amount of time for feedback. There is another extraordinary production constraint too.

Monologue- and story-readings, and audio books isolate the actor the most, with the working pair of actor and producer. There is little input from the studio manager who remains in the control cubicle. This can result in the most concentrated studio work between the producer and actor, intensely noting each phrase, with the producer alone as the 'first audience'. (See Chapter 8.) How are you to get necessary feedback for your task of 'objectification' of your performance, your 'split reality' as a performer? Of course, you have director's notes and the other players, your first audience. But does the radio production process increase the power of the director? In my observation, it can, significantly. And further – how are you to discover and test the reality of the radio scenes?

Constructing set and character for yourself – outside or inside?

Find your imaginary 'pictures' to create the set.

Find your character's 'body' and get it to work for you.

Work from the character's 'outside' and 'inside'.

Work at your character's biography and the detail.

The radio studio offers you the greatest challenge in creating character and scene setting because it offers no visual clues. You have to invent the scene's environment in your mind's eye, using your actor's imagination. The studio can seem dry and sterile, furnished in 'BBC brown' or 'BBC green', or whatever the independent facility has to offer. Acting in sound means there is no scenery, no visual clues to location, it all has to come from within. David Holt, previously actor in the RDC explains, 'Actors find it difficult to create believability in BBC studios, it's a very artificial situation. There are cue lights, fluorescent lighting. You can be asked to do the most technical things.'

There are no objects or scenery to endow with meaning, as you have been trained to do in stage acting. There are no costumes, with the rare exception of a Spot dress or chain mail, for a Renaissance play, say, and you do not inhabit a stage or film set. It is all over to your fantasy to create the meaning and the 'reality'; over to your imaging techniques, and inner resources. 'Looking back through twenty years of radio work,' says James Aubrey, 'I don't see Studio B10 or whatever. I see backstreets, a large house, Vietnam. And I see my fellow actors in costume. I can see the sky and everything.' Josephine Tewson explains, 'I see it, you've got to. The pictures come unbidden'; while Moir Leslie finds, 'it happens in my head and I just see the studio.' Angela Pleasence asked herself, 'Do I see a country road? Yes. I have an enormous sense of environment around me, though I don't pick out a particular poplar tree.'

Chapter 7, Putting it all to Work, deals with radio preparation, key questions to ask yourself and sensory techniques to help you concentrate and create places, emotions and character, and to make the most of your inner resources. There you will find radio techniques to endow the script situations with meaning and detail.

But let us take up the main question here. Where do you start building your radio character? One main way of working in stage rehearsal is 'from the outside in', meaning from the external characteristics – walk, stance, costume, props, markers of social status. This somatic approach, working from the body to the mind, was pioneered by Stanislavski in his *Building a Character*. Beryl Reid famously said that she began finding the character when she got the shoes right. Lord Olivier, who did little radio acting by the way, talked often of his working from the external approach. English acting, associated with technique and the 'cool', anti-emotionalist actor, is traditionally the external. The alternative is 'from the inside out', starting with thoughts and emotions. Taken to its extreme, *The Method* under Lee Strasberg used deep psychologizing, that resulted in 'mumblers' and over-introspective performers, according to its detractors.

Peter Barkworth, in his essential compendium *All About Acting*, says he begins with the voice for stage plays. That seems a very good place to start for radio, but is the voice 'outside' or 'inside'? Obviously there are different pathways for actors and different styles of plays, but base yourself on the axiom that the actor must integrate outside and inside, and work on the detail and reality of the character. It may seem a paradox that radio acting involves an 'outside' at all. My answer is absolutely yes, you have to communicate your character's movements, stance and 'look'.

Christian Rodska explains the unity of outside and inside for him, 'I can see the character. I stand in front of the microphone and I feel the character. I wear the character.' It is liberating, for 'in the visual media, if you don't look right, you don't quite get it'. Actor Kerry Shale recalls his earlier radio roles when he 'used to dress the part always, I used to wear the "right-coloured" shirt for the character.' But now he needs less. 'I need just the suggestion, one thing to make me feel the character. For Lenny Bruce, I brought in a pair of heavy boots. For the thriller *Deadlock,* I wore a jacket to make me feel wide in the chest, with its padding.' He got the 'six-foot lanky feel' for Eugene O'Neill's *Desire Under the Elms* by wearing cowboy boots. 'I was in *The Normal Heart* in the West End at the time and the boots came from my character there. I was instructed to bring in boots for the spot effect of walking on floorboards.'

For David Holt, actor previously on the RDC, 'Stanislavski has his place absolutely in radio acting. But there is a case or two of actors who have gone too far in radio Method and are now regarded as practically unemployable. How far do you go down the road, if you have the time for preparing? The physicality you use in Method doesn't matter to the listener, even though you can transform yourself bodily. So if it feels right for you, use it.' Alaistair McGowan regularly on the *Week Ending* team warns, 'Deep Method actors cannot respond to dialect quickly enough. I do some Method, but you have to make sure it doesn't take you over. Radio does not need the same internalizing. You have to make the face, it takes over your body, but this is not a conscious decision. Your voice will lead you into doing things you didn't intend to. A producer can say, "Hunch your shoulders", and that is all the guidance you need.'

Steve Nallon of *Spitting Image* explains how he recreates his Mrs Thatcher for radio. 'You don't do what the character won't do. When I become "Mrs Thatcher", I practise the walk and the face, so it's from the outside in. I remember my old acting teacher saw me at this and said, "That's pure Stanislavski".' Kerry Shale has read the manuals, but, 'like most actors, I've evolved methods of my own. That's especially if the part is not like me. Though I wear glasses normally, I don't wear them if it does not suit the character. I keep them off, even during the lunch break, so it helps the other actors to see me differently.' Nicola Pagett believes, 'different rules apply to radio, it's not from the outside or the inside. It's clarity that matters, to be faithful to the story. You've got to think of the lines.'

Working with Spot

Spot often work in your space – get used to them.

Don't be distracted by Spot business.

You learnt about what Spot technicians do in Chapter 1 and usually you do not get to handle the sound props. On stage or film, the hand props are the physical objects you endow with reality and meaning, not least because you have them in your grasp and as the focus of your gaze, and often the centre of your concentration. In radio the Spot technicians work these props, and not often you, because skilled timing and manipulation are demanded, requiring hands free of the script. Spot technicians must also guide the actors' moves. You may never even touch your character's newspaper, murder weapon, computer keyboard or teacup. Sometimes you do not even create your own walking 'steps' – a surprisingly difficult task anyway. Spot wears your 'shoes' and walks as you on your 'ground' (concrete slabs, wooden planks, stairs).

Working with Spot is another technique to be learned. Actors have to get used to Spot busy around them, kneeling at their feet, in their 'bed-sheets', wearing their prop 'shoes', 'clothes' and weapons, sometimes touching, moving and tugging at them, and in their space, invading their acting body space, too. At other times actors do not see the technicians when they are hidden behind a screen and recorded on a separate microphone. Do not get distracted by staring at Spot because their actions too often look surreal. Matthew Morgan got a shock at first. 'It was in the Ruth Rendell thriller, *A Fatal Inversion,* and in the scene I was watching TV with my wife. Suddenly, Spot opened up a newspaper behind me, a total symbiosis. Spot are a performance in themselves, they have a terrific level of performance energy.' Director Pam Brighton gets 'the actors to do Spot when there's a relationship with what they're doing, like digging and chopping.' John Taylor believes 'actors have to be given some sense of location and acoustic. Working with kids is a good way for the director to learn this. You have to give them props for their imagination, something concrete. So you give them a letter to open, or a phone to dial. Adult actors don't like to admit and realize they need these props. You've got to help them create the reality. Most actors will improve if given a little, not too much, to help them. The prop becomes an emblem for that imagined world, it helps them to focus.'

Director Hamish Wilson gives an example. 'It's useful for a courting couple to act when sitting down, so they can grapple. For a bed, I put sheets on the floor and the actors get under them. It helps radio actors who have to work with a paradox – that they are not supported and endorsed in creating characters by a time and a place. The radio actors have to convince themselves that such is the case of the plot situation and then convince the audience. The actor has to imagine that place first and then inhabit it.' Elizabeth Spriggs remembers playing her part of an old married couple in a bed. 'Spot brought in a decrepit, squeaky sofa and we had to bounce up and down.' Nicola Pagett explained how she died of arsenic poisoning in *Madame Bovary.* 'I brought some muesli with me for the choking effect of the poison in the famous death scene. The BBC are good with supplying props, but on this occasion they'd nothing.' However, any further experiments with props, explains John Taylor, and 'you'd be breaking the conventions of studio practice. The actors would think you are a finnicky director and become suspicious.'

Welcome to the world of language

When you get the script, you must read the whole play and not just your scenes. You have to grasp the interrelations between all the characters and have ready your answers to questions of detail that continually crop up in the studio. Under pressure, anybody can have blanks about the script, but you will oblige the production and your director if you can come up with solutions.

You have to understand the script at several levels:

Storyline with its conflicts and obstacles, and its through-line (Stanislavski).

Style, genre, theme and meaning.

Language and styles of language characters use.

Relations between the characters.

Given circumstances – the dramatic situation.

Subtext to convey the full meaning.

Thorough actor's training and an acting manual give you these fundamentals and I cannot dwell on them here. What I need to do is focus on your extra obligations to a radio play script:

Extra work if an adaptation, e.g. from a novel or stage play – read the original.

A greater sensitivity to your lines and being word-based.

How to contradict your lines on radio and make the subtext work for you.

The world of radio drama is the world of language. Radio characters are almost totally word-based rather than some stage and film characters who have a strong physical presence. These radio words speak often the languages of reason and passion, and it is for you to discover the deeper subtext and unconscious. It is radio's strength that it speaks and that it is *logic*-based – that is 'logic' as it is originally derived from the Greek for 'word' and 'reason'. It is sometimes difficult for actor and playwright on radio to reach through to the lower levels of the mind, that is, to pre-formed speech, emotion and instinct. Down there, are inner turmoil, other 'voices' of the mind, dreaming and emotions before they are formulated into finished speech.

Yet it is on the margins of words that much modern acting depends, particularly a lot of what we find exciting, sexy, popular or experimental in film and theatre: the subtext and an individual's psychology, the revealing close-up, speechless thought surfacing in face and body, inarticulate rebels. Much of twentieth-century acting technique and training has to do with opening up this last frontier – the character's mind – and often through close-ups of the face. Even viewing TV soaps you notice that some sequences are built around the reaction shots, rather than the speakers. In a sense, radio offers you clearer ground on which to work, as your main task is to get to grips with the words.

Take also the plot situation where inner emotion contradicts what is said. A stage or film actor must often indicate that what the character says is not what he or she means. But radio is about the speaker rather than the receiving listener character; there are no reaction shots on radio. Radio does not have the visual track and is not the 'theatre of the face'. Of course there is subtext in radio acting, the 'space between the words', but most of the signification must be there in the script. You have to make the subtext work for you.

The mainstream and strength of radio drama are 'talky' plays, often domestic, family-based, what the Americans call 'hearth' plays, along with adaptations of well-known novels and stage plays. It is a lived-in, approachable world. Director Pam Brighton reflects, 'I'm very lucky because I work in Ireland where the actors are happy with language and acting is mostly language-based, and where their emotional imaginations arise from words.' To sum up, radio language is omnipresent, a continuous flow of reason and explicable emotion. The radio characters have to keep on communicating, with each other and with themselves. They cannot fail – for being dumb they would become absent in this blind medium.

Description – the scripted extra in your lines

There is a special extra in radio scripts to compensate for the blind medium. Screen writers are told again and again to 'cut the words' and print journalists know that 'a picture counts for a thousand words'. But radio writers do not have that option because they have to describe and create the sound pictures themselves. Inserts have to be dropped into dialogue to put across physical details, a character's looks, expressions and movements. This is so essential to radio technique that I use the term 'description' to pin it down. Description is a rule of radio, so I call it the *There You Are On The Sofa With Your Box Of Chocolates, Irene* Rule. Just as description is technically testing for the scriptwriter so it is for the actor. How to put over some phrases so obvious and, from time to time on the page, so wooden?

No wonder actors groan about it, off microphone, because it can be one of the most artificial things they have to cope with. True, any play has to give 'the story so far' details early on, technically called exposition, and this is a tough challenge for any playwright in any medium. But radio has to insert, or drop in, description into nearly every stretch of dialogue. Though often radio drama is about doing less, because less is needed in a blind medium, here is an area where radio constantly has to do more. Another job of the playwright is often to reveal the subtextual reactions of the character, to reveal and capture in words, rather than leave them to emerge in facial reactions, as in film. Radio writing can sometimes be a series of statements about the character and not about transitions in emotions.

However, description can give strength to a scene, too, when it works in combination and earns its place in the script, and this gives the actor just what he or she needs to flesh out the character. You can tune in to lots of effective examples in *The Archers*, due to its talented stable of playwrights and script editor, Vanessa Whitburn. For example, gossipy Mrs Snell whispers jealously of a woman visitor: 'I suppose she thinks that brown-eyed stare is flattering.'

Take this skilled opening of Aileen La Tourette's *The Christening Robe*, in which description mixes its work with exposition, and you can detect how each earns its place:

1. FX:	ORGAN WEDDING VOLUNTARY AMID CONGREGATION MUTTERING.
2. OLD MAN:	[whispering intimately] I say, who's that with the bride?
3. YOUNG WOMAN:	That's Gran, you fool.
4. OLD MAN:	Whose Gran?
5. YOUNG WOMAN:	Harriet's of course. She brought her up. Shhh.

6. OLD MAN:	Harriet's the bride?
7. YOUNG WOMAN:	[sarcastically joking] No – Harriet's the vicar.
8. OLD MAN:	She might have been. There are women vicars. There might even be men called Harriet.

The exchange continues with this bantering, effective word play and of course, introduces us, via an intriguing 'hook', into the problem of a bride and her two mothers-in-law, and we get to 'see' the main characters. There is lots offered to the actors in filling in the details of the moving sound pictures. Timothy West was responsible for a glorious radio spoof which parodied the stock techniques of radio, and description among everything else, as it blazons across its title, *This Gun I have in My Right Hand is Loaded*. (Made in the Bristol studio, his 15-minute farce has never been broadcast, though it has a wide circulation as a samizdat cassette. Fortunately you can enjoy the text for yourself in Rosemary Horstmann's *Writing for Radio*. See bibliography.) Radio actors must remember there is always a second play going on – the second radio play in the mind of the listeners, playing on their 'mind-screen'. 'The audience is the final actor', as actors put it.

Reactions and the 'umms'

Use the 'grunts' and the 'umms'.

Use the 'language around language' – paralanguage.

Another addition to the scripted words is what radio actors call the 'grunts' or the 'umms'. Sometimes they say to the director, 'Do you want me to react here?' What they mean are grunts, groans, giggles, 'aahs', 'umms', breathiness, and all that fills the spaces between our words. I define two sorts of 'umms' here. Firstly, additions you can make to your scripted words to express subtext and to give colour, and secondly, reactions you make while other characters are speaking their lines. Using reactions is a controversial issue, as they can 'crash into' others' lines and get messy. They must be scripted after discussion – and marked up on your script for retakes. It is polite, indeed essential, to check them out with your fellow actors, asking 'partner, can I crash into your line here?' 'Umms' and reactions are the language around language which we use all the time in our everyday talk. The academic term for it is paralanguage. The 'para-' means 'around'. Although it is a word that crops up in linguistics textbooks and not in the studio, I will use paralanguage as a term here.

In the play I quoted from earlier, *The Christening Robe*, directed by Jane Morgan, a couple of scenes later, the bride changes into her going-away outfit, chatting confidentially with her grandmother. I have added a few production notes to the original script to give you an indication, even in this small, mid-scene excerpt, of how the 'umms' and embodying combine with positions and Spot. This far into the book, you should begin to understand how technique and creative production combine. The actresses are mostly in position 2 (intimate) and the acoustic is boxy, in a bedroom, in front of the dressing-table mirror:

1. HARRIET: OK, [breathing in and energetic] now time to take off the bridal make-up and on with the whorey stuff.

2. GRANDMOTHER: [slow, emphatic] I should go easy dear, [musing with breath in] – understatement.

3. HARRIET: [stretching face and lips, putting on make-up] Not my style, Gran. You old hypocrite!

4. FX SPOT: FIDDLING AROUND IN MAKE-UP BOX.

5. GRANDMOTHER: [position 2, very close, still slow] I should wear the same foundation pet. [Back a bit but still position 2] I noticed it when I gave you away.

6. HARRIET: Or didn't! [giggling]

7. FX SPOT: MORE ROOTING AROUND MAKE-UP BOX AND SHAKING BOTTLE.

You can see what a lot of production detail there is here, appropriate to an important point in the story, and it is economical too. Yet this is only fifteen seconds in broadcast time. Though I have to detail techniques singly, they work in combination usually. The mood of this scene comes through the paralanguage too, you get some of the subtext there, it is essential to the pair's rhythm, and the contrast and intimacy between them. Paralanguage is part of how the actors 'live in' the lines, it all has to be appropriate and timed, and there can be no wasteful 'umms'. There is no language without paralanguage. As an experiment, try the short scene you have just read without paralanguage, and see how it loses colour.

There can be great use of the 'umms' and reactions in radio comedy (for example, the 'Oowww' in Kenneth Williams' catch phrase, 'oowww, stop messing about') and in extending character types, such as the alcoholic (mumbling, yawning), the old fusspot (rapid repetitions, false starts, breathiness, clacking lips), the happy-go-lucky (humming, giggling), and dialect (the Yorkshire 'eee', the Cockney 'oi', the Liverpudlian 'hey'). But there is a limit to how many 'oohs', 'hahs', 'ahas', gasps and sighs, inbreaths and outbreaths, an actor can insert into his lines. Often it is just not appropriate and holds up the rhythm and cues.

Director Penny Gold is for a ban. 'I will not have "umms" and "aahs", I do not approve of people not reading what's on their scripts. If the script is unwieldy, then we can discuss changes.' Similarly, Hilary Norrish, director in the BBC World Service, thinks, 'Nothing is worse than the actor who responds to each sentence with an appropriate grunt.' Gordon House, also of BBC World Service: 'Reactions? I've done everything. Anything to avoid the unreal ping-pong effect. Sometimes having the actors talking over one another. All you do and know is that instinctively that doesn't work. The finest is the silence between words and not to be wary as a director of going for just that. Take David Suchet and Ian Holm in *The Kreutzer Sonata* I directed – silences, and struggling to get the words out. After all, you can alter the pacing in post-production, with the razor blade and the Audiofile (computer digital system).' Gordon points here to one of the most famous aspects of radio dialogue, the silences. 'You begin to understand radio acting when you create different silences.' There is even the skilled technique of suggesting the character is listening.

Patrick Rayner summarizes: 'A radio actor should even hear with his body, with a sniff, a light cough, a verbal shrug. A good actor can keep "in" the scene all the time and doesn't have to lever the character up each time he speaks.' For Ned Chaillet, director, 'Reactions come with the role. Some actresses do a lot of breathing which can be useful. Other times, actors are over-acting, but it does depend on the writing. Richard Nelson, the American playwright, for example, works in the studio with actors on his plays and loves them to live in the lines.'

But there are dangers in voicing reactions during other actors' lines. Alaistair McGowan again: 'I learnt in comedy sketches always to remind the listener of your presence. You put these noises in during another character's long speech. Some actors are more traditional and don't like it, they think you steal their thunder. But I look on it as natural.' Jonathan Taffler: 'I tend to be hesitant because you feel about the other actors, it's their bit now. And you are grunting during their speeches. But when I teach radio acting, I always get the students to do reactions.' Directors can have worries about requesting reactions, as Caroline Raphael explains, 'Usually, asking actors to react is a disaster. You've got to say to the other actor, "Don't wait for them." By making a call for reactions, you give a different flow to the dialogue and the actors start to cue themselves differently.'

Reactions are needed at times, according to John Taylor, 'especially for a love scene. That depends on two people doing the same thing and where what is said is much less important than what's felt. Lovers' breathing can be erotic on radio, it's intimacy and closeness.' Finally, Patrick Rayner puts the case for using reactions, 'I prefer to keep the actors acting all the time, because it's about them listening, and not all reading. A seasoned pro might wander away, though still meant to be in the scene, to turn a page quietly or to scratch his bum behind the curtain.' Also, Alaistair McGowan: 'You can't "miss out on a moment". You take it in and then react. You have to make those little noises. It bridges the moment. If you come in too quickly on cue, all you've got is on the paper. It [an umm] gives the listener time to catch up.' You have to give the listeners time to catch up and not just by pauses. On the film lot, an actor who cannot react for the camera is called 'frozen face'. You must not become a radio 'frozen throat'.

Interiorizing or 'thoughts'

'Interiorizing' is the scripted inner monologue.
Try focusing on the point between your eyebrows.

Radio has another strength. It can reach deep within the speaking mind and broadcast the running 'monologue' inside a character. This is the 'me' inside the outer shell of the 'I'. In this respect among others, it can claim to extend its frontier further than plays in other media. I call this radio technique, that of opening out the speaking mind, 'interiorizing'. This 'interiorizing' I term radio's 'fifth dimension' and to record it you are usually close-miked, in positions 1 or 2, and heard by the listeners in your acoustic alone. If it is a lengthy monologue, perhaps the whole play, you are more likely to be in position 3. It is where radio is essentially radiogenic. Radio can also flip over to a totally subjective scene and inhabit itself in that area of the mind where the character's thoughts become ours by broadcast transference.

Interiorizing demands the skill of turning your character inside out. The sort of person who lives so intensely in their mind is usually what is called a 'stretched' character, with unbalanced emotions and experiences. Monologues like that give you a lot to work on and there is one technique I have to offer that may be useful. To find your focus of attention for this interior work, try concentrating on the point between your eyebrows. Touch it to find and explore it, and touch it again to remind yourself of this point of concentration. This is where some believe your 'third eye' is, a focus for meditation. It is also a chakra point, one of the points of energy in the body. No matter whether you are New Age or not, try this technique of focusing all your energy on to one point and making it the entrance into the depths of your mind.

Narrator

Radio is also the ideal medium for the narrator frame, the story-voice, which we often hear in a neutral acoustic. The narrator can be written as a character within the story, the protagonist keeping a diary, for example, and so subjective; or the narrator can be objective, the 'voice-of-God' commentator. The Radio 4 Classic Serial, adaptations of great novels, often uses the commentator, the authorial voice descended from the nineteenth-century realist novel tradition. The listeners are given an objective vantage-point over the play events, a technique we also know from the story-voice of classic *film noir*. You need the same skills as narrator as you use for story-reading: precision and style. Usually, all the narrator's scenes are recorded together.

In all you do, dialect, emphasis and pronunciation have to be precise because radio is totally an ear, or aural, medium. The director knows listeners are more likely to write in about language than about the play's quality or content. There should be time to pick up on even a single word in a retake and iron it out in post-production, whereas in other media, you sometimes hear fluffs, or verbal mistakes – in TV soaps for example.

Fluffs and other hazards

When you fluff, go back and repeat from the top of the sentence. For the takes, repeat your performance accurately.

An advantage for the radio actor is that the recording process can be interrupted relatively easily, with little or no cost to the production other than time. This removes some of the fear of 'fluffs', or verbal mistakes. The studio rule is: when you make a fluff, leave a few seconds – for later tape editing – and then resume from the top of the sentence. Fluffs are not unusual and getting over them in this professional way causes the minimum of interruption. There is a lot of stopping and starting, anyway, for technical reasons from within the control cubicle. Do not say, 'Where do you want me to go back to?' You may go back further if you need a run at it, for example with tension creeping into the voice.

You should get more confidence from noting that fluffs are mainly three types in origin. You can misread something, like 'orgasm' for 'organism', and that is a matter of concentration. Then you can suffer the tongue-slip such as the spoonerism, 'patter-killer' instead of 'caterpillar'. Charlotte Green, the Radio 4 newsreader, once said 'cross flannel cherry' for 'cross-Channel ferry'. The right items have been assembled in your mind but emerge in the wrong order. Another type of fluff is where you misread 'capital punishment' for 'corporal punishment'. You have accidentally picked a closely related but wrong word from the word recognition store in your mental dictionary. You might jokingly be accused of a 'Freudian slip', based on Freud's claim that slips of the tongue betray suppressed thoughts.

Like the film actor, the radio actor has to repeat exactly his performance for each retake, especially the timing. This may be essential, for example, if grams is mixing in an FX at a precise point. Another advantage is that there need not be many takes. Actors are usually not told why there was a hold-up, as there is not time to explain the details into the studio. The director will merely say, 'Sorry everybody, got to retake – technical problems'. But if all goes well, the director may 'buy' the first take, that is, he decides he has got all he needs, and does not need a second take. So on you go to the next sequence. The actor has to be up to the fatigue of retakes and it can be demoralizing if it gets to the sixth and beyond. This is where an accurate memory is needed, for an exact repetition in timing, voicing and moves, allowing for any adjustments the director has requested in his notes. If a word or so is out of place, a retake could be as little as a single word, phrase or a line. The actor has to be able to pitch that retake accurately, so that it can later be 'dropped in', during post-production editing. An actor who is ill-prepared or erratic will not be up to these demands. As in all production, the creative magic can work the first time round, or even on the sixth or seventh take. But there is a law of diminishing returns due to fatigue.

Standing around

There are other hazards lurking in the script. You may be a minor, often third, party in a dialogue with few lines for you and these have little or no lead-in to them. That is, there is little or no build to cue them in, and they have little place overall in the rise and fall of the scene dialogue, or so it could seem to you. You could be a waiter for example, a cameo role, or the neglected husband, or the drop-in neighbour. Such 'isolated' phrases are difficult to make convincing; they make little 'islands' of their own on the page. You as actor are left standing in between stretches of dialogue, and 'standing' in radio means fading out to invisibility from the memory of the listener. You can try to maintain 'presence' once or twice, if you can, by paralanguage (see page 86), but you might have to create another mini-*entrance* for a phrase. You do this by an intake of breath, before the first scripted word, only if appropriate. Otherwise you are drawing too much attention to yourself, 'up-microphoning' in fact! Subtleties like these short, solitary phrases expose a radio actor's technique and are quite a test in your training. But there are no 'walk-ons' in the radio scene. You have to make all your lines do their work.

Tops and Tails

The tops and tails of radio scenes provide more perils, partly because there are so many of them. *The Archers* has about seven scenes in an episode of fifteen minutes, and a half hour of a radio play can have say, ten to twenty scenes. If it is comedy, and this leads us on to discuss styles, you usually bring up the end of the scene brightly and a good playwright will give you the script to work with. The top of a scene is often mid-conversation, because radio has an advantage here. It neither has to transport characters into the middle of a stage space, nor does it need as much 'scene establishing' as TV and film location shots. It is more economical and can deliver the listeners into the middle of the situation. For scene tops, you have to have the feel of what went on just before, the 'pre-life' of the dialogue, and judge your pacing. Again, listen in to *The Archers* for examples of tops and tails.

A typical top is, 'Not finished digging those carrots yet, Tony?' This has description, exposition, location and it demands a response from Tony. Or Elizabeth says teasingly to Nigel, 'A fine way to treat a lady,' and that gives a spurt to the dialogue. An example of a tail, one of the many, is, 'After all, that's all you give a baby – love,' is a satisfying epigram to round off an emotional exchange with the widowed Shula. Chapter 7 will give preparation techniques to get you through these difficulties.

You will also be asked to double up in crowd scenes and again, the microphone picks up the slightest word or phrase. Take care to get your contribution scripted – most directors are especially precise and detailed about this. The reason for going to the trouble of recording crowd scenes, and not just taking them off a pre-recorded effects CD, is that it gets the play's period more creatively, and you avoid what Jane Morgan calls 'the standard crowd of dervishes'. And don't offer 'rhubarb' in a revolutionary mob or the Roman forum!

Chapter 6
Voice

From the *Lawrence of the Arctic* sketch in *I'm Sorry I'll Read That Again*

Bill Oddie:	(playing Nanook of the North, but in broad Yorkshire) How do 'ee, by gum, it's right gradely to see 'ee, have a chip buttie—
FX:	REFEREE'S WHISTLE BLOWN
John Cleese:	Wrong voice!
Bill Oddie:	Now listen, beanpole, I'm playing Nanook of the North and this is a Northern accent I'm doing. So you can like it or you can lump it!

Your product is your voice. This chapter aims to top up your professional voice training and manuals, and your daily voice exercises; and to explain how you adapt your voice for radio. There are three sections:

How voice is produced – the voice mechanism.

Five aspects of the voice for radio: pitch, volume and breathing, tempo, voice qualities, dialect.

Your voice doctor for radio, and relaxation.

I give some basic information that may be familiar to you, but it always bears repeating. As I mentioned in the introduction, I take up from when your voice is in readiness and advanced in development. You need to work under professional teachers and gain an objectivity in analysing your voice product, and to go back for instruction to top up your skills and dialect work. You can also get a voice check for imperfections, mannerisms and bad habits that might have crept in. Here a cassette and microphone are indispensable to give you immediate feedback, and make you feel more in control of your voice. Then you will balance words and meaning, with spontaneity as you 'lift it off the page'.

Richard Griffiths, actor:

It seems to me that everybody's 'voice' is either six inches extended out from the mouth or as much as six inches back into the mouth. With an outgoing personality, it's six inches out. When I acted Hitchcock as a radio character, his voice is pushed right to the back, he's secretive, retentive, you've got to approach his voice in a psychological way. He's like Kissinger speaking. Most people have their 'voice' where it should be, on their lips or beyond. It's not to do with loudness or confidence. It's to do with the mind's eye, deciding where the centre of gravity of a voice should be.

Steve Nallon, actor:

I feel my own voice is about one inch inside my mouth. Take Simon Fanshawe, the stand-up comedian, he's an outgoing personality, his is six inches out!

Liane Aukin, director:

I once cast a wonderful actor and discovered too late that all the expressiveness was in his face not the voice. It's upsetting for the actor too, because he can't understand why he's not getting the role.

How voice is produced – the vocal mechanism

Larynx = voice box situated at the top of the windpipe.

Vocal cords = two small, tough folds in the larynx that vibrate and so cause the actual sounds we make.

Men have thicker and longer vocal bands than most women, and more bass than treble. They measure between 22–32 mm (1¼–⅞ in.) in men, while in women, between 12–22mm (⅞–½ in.). The average fundamental frequency for male voices is 128 cycles or Hz (waves) per second. For women it is higher, at 200-256 cycles or Hz. Below this is relevant in differentiating characters' voices in a scene and avoiding what I call 'clustering' where it is difficult for the listener to pick out who is who.

Diaphragm = muscle separating the thorax from the abdomen. When it descends, breath is drawn into the lungs – important in power-training for breath.

Most speech results from a rising column of air, produced by the lungs, diaphragm and bronchial tubes which act as a 'bellows'. This is the exhaling breath, the outbreath. Voicing is also achieved through inhaling breath, the inbreath, as in heaving and shock sighs, 'aahs', useful for establishing presence. As an experiment, try the different screams produced by your outbreath and inbreath. Then try a slight sigh, feeling the difference between out and in, and as if at position 1 at the microphone. You have to be aware and in control of the detail.

In ordinary speech we use half, or less, of the breath force, and we do not develop muscles in this bellows system to their full potential. Actors' training extends the diaphragm and the whole vocal system, maximizing vocal technique by stance and efficient use of energy. The radio actor needs all this and more, working long days standing at the microphone. You also have to control the breath force for low volume, at effective low power, for accurate phrasing, and to avoid blasting and popping. Most radio acting is at low levels of breathing as opposed to the throw and projection of the stage voice. As an efficient actor, you exercise your voice daily so it is precisely responsive and sustains energy. You should arrive at the studio for the morning call with a well-oiled voice. It should help to learn some technical vocabulary of the voice and talk.

FIVE ASPECTS OF THE VOICE FOR RADIO

> **Pitch or range** (also intonation = the notes in the voice.)
>
> **Volume or loudness (projection) and breathing.**
>
> **Tempo or rate (with word strike).**
>
> **Voice qualities.**
>
> **Dialect.**

Pitch or range

Pitch is the singing aspect or the melody of the voice. It is also called intonation. In speaking, the voice glides from sound to sound with an almost continuous change in pitch and this is crucial to making sense. While ordinary speech is limited, often to about five notes in range, extended emotion can widen out to fifteen notes. An actor should train up to three octaves, twenty-four notes, and wider expression in dialogue should straddle eight notes. The voice has more gradations than the notes of the musical scale, of course.

Pitch is wide or narrow: the result of the frequency of vibration of the vocal cords (folds). The well-known Laver scheme lists a 5-point scale: very deep, deep, medium, high, very high.

Clustering: Female voices have a narrower pitch range and any group of actors, male or female, can *cluster* (my term). This is a 'sameness', or overlapping, in voices and it is best avoided by initial casting, or, in the studio, by how characters, male and female, can be made to differ.

Clustering causes an 'identity crisis' in the radio play because listeners get confused by these too-similar voices. It is not due only to pitch, of course, but to what comes over as 'clone' voice qualities. The fact is we have the brain mechanics to recognize and remember visually up to 10,000 faces, but we do not have the same ability with voices unlinked to faces. Radio has a tendency to cluster, and just think how 'clonish' middle-ranking politicians sound in Radio 4 interviews. And remember how difficult it can be to recognize telephone voices when you take a call. Young actors especially are prone to what is called 'pitching up', copying fellow actors' voice patterns. The director will say, 'Can you pitch that down a bit?' or 'You're sounding a bit like X.' A problem in 'clustering' is often the reason a director demands a radical adjustment to your character (a change in dialect, age, introducing other voice qualities such as huskiness). As the cast first starts rehearsing, and from the read-through, the actor has to 'tune' his or her character against the others and that may require careful notes from the director. You need a good, trained ear and speed.

Intonation contours: Pitch variations in real-life speech creates interesting patterns in melody. These collections of notes are significant. They can create different meanings for the same phrases, for example. They are systematic, and each language and dialect has a limited stock. The technical term is intonation. An expert textbook is O'Connor & Arnold, *Intonation of Colloquial English, a practical handbook* (Longman 1961) which types ten 'tone groups'. We study these patterned variations as *intonation contours* in sentences and they are important in actors' training. It is useful to think of them as contour lines on a map showing altitude (valleys and hills). A simple declaring sentence ends with a falling contour, and questions anticipating a 'Yes' or a 'No', finish with a rise. American-English gives the speaker a great deal of freedom in intonation.

Optimum pitch: Each of us has our own *habitual pitch*. This is the middle of our pitch range, though not necessarily a clearly fixed point. You will find voice teachers differ as to whether there is a defined centre or whether it fluctuates. Jacqueline Martin explains in *Voice in the Modern Theatre*, p.39 (Routledge, 1991), 'Scientists have determined that an individual's natural pitch level, which is often referred to as "optimum", lies somewhere near the third or fourth tone above the lowest which can be produced clearly.' In *Speech and Hearing Science* pp.182–3 (Englewood Cliffs, NY, 1968), W. Zemlin says, 'the natural pitch is located about one-fourth up the total singing range (including falsetto), when the range is expressed in musical notes.'

What matters is that you have a 'well-oiled' range and that you bring the concept of *habitual pitch* to your discovery of the character. This gives you an advantage, you have something else to work on for characterization: the character's 'middle' and habitual range, the most frequent notes he or she uses, and how far that character can travel with the voice.

Another reason for using this precise discovery is that individuals most often begin speaking on or around that middle note, it is where your character takes up the cue. Although some voice teachers argue against training around your own habitual pitch because you might find this restricts your potential, it is certainly useful to think of the characters you are creating as each having an habitual pitch, the 'middle' or 'centre' for their voice and personality. Using technical terms like these enables you to map out your acting tasks, to appraise them and to problem-solve, rather than solely relying on an actor's instinct and common sense.

Pitch and position: Pitch will 'go' differently to the microphone depending on your position. Close to the microphone, positions 1 and 2 bring out the bass notes. Position 1 for you can differ to position 1 for another. Directors also solve the boominess problem by putting actors on separate microphones, 'miking separately'.

Liane Aukin, director:
You have to go for variety in casting, high and low – if you only liked one voice it would be fatal!

The most frequently-heard criticism of radio acting is that it sounds flat and wooden. Monotony for the listener will not always be due to lack of pitch variation in the character, it has to do with pace too, and other aspects. But pitch variation or contours are often the best starting-point.

Liane Aukin comments, 'A woman can lighten her voice and what matters is the quality. I find women's voices are increasing in range and diversity. As women get older, their voices are more distinctive, more personal, lived in. Young girls are the hardest. My toughest casting was a Colette play, with twelve schoolgirls. The solution was they were strong types, wonderfully characterized. Problems are solved by talking it through or by looking at the part in a different way, it's the director's problem, and a booboo may have been made initially.'

It is generally felt that listeners find lower-pitched women's voices more attractive, especially when they are husky and sexy, and contrast with other attractive female voices. Mrs Thatcher successfully went through a training programme, with a teacher from the National Theatre, to lower her pitch. It included special humming exercises. Scientific tape analysis of her speeches before and after, shows she reduced her pitch by 46 Hz, almost half the average difference between male and female voices. She also slowed down a bit, as we tend to reduce word speed when we lower pitch in talk. Women's voices also rise and fall with age, and alter with the menopause. There is also a steady reduction up to age 45 and after this the pitch gradually rises again.

There are times when a flatness and repetition of a flattened-out *intonation contour* suits a scene. It all depends on what the script offers and how much emotion is convincing and appropriate. In real-life talk, we know that emotion uses higher or lower tones. Anger, fear, hysteria, nervousness and tension go high. Going low means grief, love, sincerity. Conversation is set in the middle register. You have to suit the pitch to the play's style and it should be useful to check a character against the ten-plus acting styles I list in Chapter 7. In the adaptation of a well-known stage play such as a Coward, Shakespeare or Shaw, the *crossover*-classic style predetermines the range. In the mainstream English tradition, stage speech patterns are set and determined in many ways. There is the rule of playing through to the end of the phrase, for example.

Liane Aukin, director:
It's not necessarily the voice going up and down that tells you what is in the mind of the character, or not in their mind.

What goes wrong with pitch, and some solutions

A repetitive intonation pattern, especially a flat contour
The problem here is that the actor may be unaware of annoyingly repetitive or flat patterns or that his/her choices are inadequate. For listeners, the actor's delivery comes over as monotonous and boring if he never moves off those few notes. Equally a problem are 'repeated tunes' as Morrison terms them in *Clear Speech*, p.27. Young actors

are prone to these repetitive patterns across a phrase and they are particularly noticeable at the end of sentences, where usually the 'tune' has a fall. It is called the 'Low Fall ending' by O'Connor & Arnold in *Intonation of Colloquial English*, p.13. Any of these 'tunes' can become infuriating to the listener if it is obvious that the actor is not 'thinking through', balancing meaning and words.

Monotonous range

This is the radio character who is boxed in by the script. Being a boring character in a radio play is to be boring squared. You have to think about possible ways around this before you go into the studio, because you cannot rely on the director for everything. Go for other aspects of the voice and get 'on' to the words.

Repetitive dialect patterns

This is a tough problem because non-standard dialects have distinctive 'repeated tunes', especially those with a Celtic base, and they contrast with the flatness of received-pronunciation (RP) English. It makes them even more attractive for the listener, the tunes are part of the pleasure, but actors must ring the changes. Again, this can be more of a problem with young actors and the inexperienced. Examples are the Londonderry and Newcastle dialects, seemingly with a 'High Rise ending' for every phrase, and the 'Rise-Fall' of the Shetlands. An actor who is uncertain about a foreign accent, New York say or Parisian, might clutch at 'repeated tunes' to get through longer passages, but it comes over as a sign of weakness. Again, sentence endings and where you come to the end of your cue are danger areas as you are likely to be exposed there. You should not offer a dialect which just fits where it hits – your character has to live in it.

Straining the character's optimum pitch

This is where the character's range poses a strain for you anyway. For example, the sexy 'baby-doll' high notes, the 'coloratura' sweeping up and down the octaves, and the 'Old Man Ribba' pushing your voice down too low. Laurence Olivier added a whole octave in the bass for *Othello* in 1964 at the Old Vic. It took him five months with a professional teacher, typical of his technical inventiveness. You do the best you can, know your range and keep 'oiled'.

Avoid the 'voice beautiful'

Through the last thirty years to today, the debate in staging Renaissance Theatre continues between music and meaning, naturalism and declamation. You will find a full discussion of this in Martin and Berry (see the bibliography). There are very few stars with 'classic' pitch performances. Sir John Gielgud, whose voice was described as an 'Elizabethan oboe' is one famous example, and Robert Eddison, who died in 1991, was another, a marvellous radio actor whose vocal 'key' was high tenor, soaring through long phrases.

You need to sharpen your technique by exercises. Do some observation on 'tunes', not just on radio plays, but by listening critically to local radio news and the 'inserts' of various correspondents reporting, especially on sport. You could note their intonation contours on paper, as an exercise. Many of the reporters adopt repeated tunes as style, with alternating 'Low Fall ending' and 'High Rise ending'.

I suggest local radio stations, because you will hear such a wide range of voices. Think what you would do, reading the same scripts. What is effective and what is not? English has only a limited number of pitch patterns and it is a matter of using them recurrently but with adequate variety. Of course you must also listen to radio plays concentrating on pitch techniques. Listen for intonation contours, the habitual pitch for each character, optimum pitch, and where pitch expresses emotion, along with peak emotions. Identify the acting style of the play, perhaps from the ten-plus acting styles given in Chapter 7. Listen for emotion and pitch, and the interesting strains to high and low.

Check list: pitch

Habitual pitch = the middle of your pitch range, and the character's.

Intonation contours = the patterned variations in sentences.

Repetitive intonation pattern = a monotonous and repeating pitch pattern in your phrases and sentences.

Optimum pitch = the range of notes in a character's voice.

Clustering = two or more characters sound too alike.

Volume or loudness, and breathing

The Laver system, which is a descriptive guide to the voice, gives a 5-point volume scale: very soft, soft, medium, loud, very loud. To invent a scale for radio acting would need more gradations, especially on the soft or low end of the spectrum, for positions 1 to 3. The voicing does not go as forcefully at the loudness end, especially when shouting 'off' the microphone, in moves or behind screens. The mechanism for volume is in the mouth and is used to vary the vocal cavities, with the lips, tongue, etc. This forces or relaxes the stream of sound. It involves breathing techniques.

Radio technique is always a matter of subtlety and the smaller effect. We call the projection needed for a theatre, 'enlargement', and it has the dangers of overplaying. Radio brings the actor closer to the essentials of playing, sensitive to the word and to the character's inner states. There is the danger that the radio actor does strain and psychologically, or from faulty technique, 'enlarges' at the microphone, 'is too big'. Hilary Norrish, director, warns, 'There's a sort of panic in some radio actors. If they don't make themselves heard, they think they are not felt by the listener. They need to control.' Actor Fraser Kerr explains, 'One of my biggest hurdles is playing a loud-voiced character, because the mike can't take it. You force your voice, if you mistake it. It's technically hell – you have to give the impression of a big booming voice, otherwise, you go over the top.' Anna Gilbert also says, 'It's not how much puff you have, like getting to the end of a dance routine. It's about how you control your breath in the closest detail.'

At the other end of the scale, you have to control whispering, breathing and your inbreath and outbreath. You are particularly exposed when you have to establish presence, the least way being with a swift inbreath. Or the script signals you to give a grunt of exertion, perhaps struggling with a garden spade or a car engine. You have arrived, naturalized your entry and covered your movement into the sound picture. Often it is as you shift from position 4 to position 3 at the microphone and make your approach.

It could be more emphatic, particularly at the top of the scene and indicating a peak emotion. Take this example, where you are the distressed partner:

1. WIFE: [HALF-SOBBING, OPENS FRIDGE DOOR AND RIFLES THROUGH CONTENTS. IN POSITION 2]

2. HUSBAND: [ARRIVING DOWN INTO KITCHEN]
I'm leaving you. I can't stand this sleeplessness any more.

3. WIFE: [SOBS]

Check list: volume and breathing

Be in complete control and know how your breathing goes to the microphone – on radio this is a miniaturist art. You do not need to fill the space, as in theatre.

Get to know the detail of your vocalizing: incoming and outgoing sounds (the inbreath and the outbreath), rhythms and your paralanguage 'vocabulary' of breathing. Also how breathing through the nose or the mouth is distinctive. Don't be a 'closet' snuffler, it will read on the microphone.

Master the ultimate in miniature – establishing presence solely through breathing. Breath is your pathway to more sophisticated radio acting.

Hyperventilating situations – running on the spot, lifting – will test you in studio conditions. Don't get tested to destruction!

When do you breathe in for your cue? Learn by experience and know that the microphone picks up everything. Sometimes you need a turn.

Liane Aukin, director:
It's all done on breath. Because you need so little voice on radio, it's mostly a low level breathing, almost as if in sleep. Then, if passion is needed, you use more. The sound of breath on the microphone is one of the sexiest things in this world.

Hilary Norrish, director:
Go for the subtleties – range and breath. I feel you need an entire chapter on breath itself, it's not just the stage techniques. It goes from the catch in the throat which means 'I can't believe that you've just said that'. And then the actor has to have a closed throat before the next sentence. The radio actor has to remember this – it's important: if you over-pitch, over-emote, under-emote, if you are lazy, nothing is more apparent.

Correct breathing allows flexibility, relaxation and optimum efficiency. Again, it is over to your regular training and exercises. But a useful extension for you as an actor is to record your breathing 'vocabulary', as listed above. You need good technical equipment for this with adequate recording levels. Laver describes some breathing types as nasalized, denasalized, with forward lips, with raised larynx and muffled. Hyperventilating – gasping for breath after rapid movement – is a danger, and Fraser Kerr recalls the days of mono, when plays went out live. 'I'm running through grass in this scene and then I have to rush over to the narration mike and do two pages. My head's spinning. The solution nowadays of course, with recording separate scenes, is to do the narration before the rapid movement.'

Tempo or rate with word strike

This is the speed of voice production, fast or slow, and of course it is linked to overall phrasing, the rhythm of a dialogue sequence and breath control. But with radio and voice-over work, tempo or rate merits a special place. For readings and commercials, the producer will often require you to speed up and fit in more words per minute. You should be able to mark up your script for this and to reckon timings before and in the studio.

Word strike is a measure of pace – the number of words counted per minute. It records crudely the speed of word delivery. The average for lively speech, in real-life talk, is 120-140 words per minute (wpm), and slowing down to 90-100 wpm can reveal incapacity, deep emotion, dignity, or a speaker's desire to 'hold the floor', all depending on the context. In book readings on Radio 4, such as *A Book At Bedtime*, the pace is normally 150 wpm. Word strike is a mechanical measurement only, since all depends on the context of the dialogue. Comedy, especially monologues, demands speed in articulation. John Cleese in his *I'm Sorry I'll Read That Again* monologues reached up to 200 wpm. Arthur English the 'patter' comedian was famous for achieving 400 wpm. Increased word strike can indicate happiness, energy and anger. Decreased word strike is for depression, solemnity, fatigue, the elderly and shock.

Radio dialogue depends on a continuous voice stream – this is what is so special about it. There is only so long a pause can be sustained whatever the context, before it misleads the listeners into reading it as a 'fade to black' (the end of the scene) or as 'dead air'. Since the standard 'black' silence between scenes is 2 to 3 seconds, that gives the outer limit for the normal pause. Time and silences expand and contract on radio, because it is 'dramatic time'. Within measured limits, it all depends on the rhythm and situation of the scene, and style. This concentration of audience attention is called 'intensification'. In *The Archers*, Caroline's adulterous hedgeside kiss with Brian Aldridge, spied on by a shocked Tony Archer, seemed endless, it suspended the listeners' time clocks!

There are key, intensified 'moments' which require split-second timing, especially when taking up cues and in high emotion. It is useful to break up a second into tenths – decaseconds. You can mark timings, just for exercises and your observation as decaseconds, for example, 0.8 sec = 8 decaseconds. When you sense that an actor has come in too slowly on cue, it can be no more than 0.5 decaseconds, but they all count. However, it is not polite or professional to come in on top of the previous actor's lines. You could be directed to do this, of course. But if you want to propose it and it seems a good choice for your character, as I mentioned before, you request, 'Can I crash in on your line here?' 'Crash in on' is the technical term to use.

Your use of timing means creating overall phrasing and the time intervals between phrases, important also for breathing. It can also be referred to as duration. The actor has to vary between fluency and sharpness of speech, between relaxation and urgency, and always to push through to the end of the phrase. The danger lies in shallowness, both of breath, of duration and of thought, and in lack of variation.

As we know more about the science of acoustics, we have discovered the ear's perception of time is more exact than that of the eye in registering change. It perceives variations of loudness, duration, sound intensity and timbre which follow on each other with short time delays. The ear is limited in other respects, obviously because it cannot focus in the way the eye lens does, but it can detect, with great sharpness, minimum time variations in rhythm. Timing means rhythm and you will discover your character's typical speech patterns. There is also the rhythm of each scene. The playwright should offer you a scene where there are peaks and troughs, a rising and falling you could plot on a graph.

Penny Gold, director:
The pace is usually the director's fault.

Jane Morgan, director:
'Pace not race' was a famous adage of director Norman Wright. You don't have to charge through a scene to gain a sense of liveliness.

The sounds of silence

Learning the rhythms of radio also means knowing how to trust silence. There are many sorts of silence, as is often said in the studio. Of course you must be guided by the other actors and your director, but you have to have the confidence to make the silences work for you. Chapter 7 deals with 'staying in' or 'keeping in' –

how to keep up concentration and the impression for the listener that you are still in the scene when others are speaking, that your character still has presence. Sometimes this means voicing reactions during others' lines, the 'umms'. Often it means making the pauses and silences signify your presence.

But radio does not allow you to pause and to think as on stage, to take in what your character has just heard before you let your thoughts out. However old-fashioned it may appear to a stage actor, you have to pick up your cues smartly, to 'bite the cue' as they call it in American filming. Otherwise, you can leave open a yawning gap and let the scene's energy escape. One sort of silence can be the crisis of peak emotion. The unconscious or the 'me' deep inside your character is in turmoil, of grief, joy, shock, or the protective and passive numbing when too much has happened. Other silences are of anger, threat, fear, when characters are in starkly dominant-subordinate pairs. You must show the listener what then emerges from the silence, as words come to give definition to the turmoil within, when your character's 'I' takes over from the 'me'. A pause is the short gap in your character's voice stream. It serves to vary the rate of speech and to split it up into sense units, and can be used, with care, to individualize. As a general rule, repeated interruptions in the voice mechanism come over badly on radio, particularly the stammer. Try not to get lumbered with it. The listeners won't thank you for it – though that is only my opinion.

There are three further sorts of pauses to note. You use the pause to indicate subtext (such as hesitation, suspicion, affection, dominance or subordination) and emphasis. Also there is the gap before an unusual word or a name, something that happens to us often in real-life talk when we go briefly silent for word retrieval from our store. It is another strong character marker. Allied to this is the 'planning pause', where, after a phrase, or in a more complicated sentence construction, or at a comma or full stop, we mentally route the way ahead. Again, make your observations from real life. Your character's pauses are essential to building your role. A technique used by director Jeremy Mortimer is 'to slow the whole scene down in rehearsal till it's positively embarrassing for the actors so they can feel the silences, and what their character is going to say next'.

Voice qualities

These are the distinctive qualities that individualize everyone's voice. They are what make you instantly recognize a friend's voice.

The problem with definition is that there is not much of an agreed descriptive vocabulary. In technical terms, voice qualities refer to the complexity of the sound wave produced by the voice mechanism, the overtones and the partials. They are the result too of resonance, or the 'resonator mechanism' – the vocal cavities distributed around the head and throat, especially in the nose, mouth and throat (pharynx). The skilled speaker uses these to select and suppress overtones.

In radio drama, we refer mostly to a voice's 'colour'. The voice that has been 'lived in' has more overtones and lots more colour. Actors say it is due to gin and cigarettes, but with ageing, the vocal cords change. They become flabby, and also either drier or moister. Voices of some older actors on radio are the richest to listen to. For example, they can make the most of them in extended slower tempo, something many younger actors could not bring off so well. Breathing is different too, with more overtones. The best known attempt to label voice qualities comes from Laver: normal, breathy, creaky, whispery, croaky, falsetto, harsh, mellow, fluent and booming, among others. Everywhere, voices are described and categorized, for casting and for directing notes and for commercials, and you get to hear an odd vocabulary. Voice qualities are always linked with other aspects of the voice, especially pitch and the 'centre' of the character's voice. Consider Nicky Henson, Joanna Lumley, Anna Massey who all use a lower pitch setting and are immediately recognizable on radio.

Liane Aukin, director:
I can't say I like a voice, it's about whether it is expressive.

DIALECT

Dialect is only part of the 'clothing' the voice wears, of how your character appears to listeners. Your character's dialect, once you have done your voice work, tells 'at a glance' so much information about which groupings you belong to, for example:

Geographical region: a particular south London suburb, Preston not Blackpool, Chicago, sci-fi Mars, medieval Paris, town versus country, etc.

Social class: middle-class with received pronunciation (RP) or middle-class and non-RP, or even a Roman tax-collector, etc.

Sex: men and women speak differently to one another; so do daughters and mothers, etc. Transsexual and homosexual voices also can be heard to have distinctive sounds.

Age: Durham old-age pensioner, teenagers in a Bristol street, or a character going from youth to old age, etc.

Style: educated, streetwise, with a drug habit, ancient Greek peasant, hitchhiker of the galaxy, etc.

Subgroup: especially in an enclosed environment that has its own code of language such as prison, hospital, factory, heretics in hell, etc.

Dialect is the speech of groups and subgroups, and these crisscross each other, so dialect includes standard or 'correct' English and non-standard English, regional slang, patois, and formal and alternative grammar. Every character in a play and every person in real life speaks their own dialect, usually their own mixture from the groups to which they belong and as suits their present environment. In dialect studies, a single individual's speech is called a 'lect'. Any radio script, worth its broadcast time, should present your character's 'lect' on the page, strongly individualized, and that is where your task of discovery begins.

Most often an actor is cast for a skill in a particular dialect, or *cast authentically* as it is called, particularly as BBC plays are produced from strong regional bases (Belfast, Edinburgh and Glasgow, Birmingham). Constant training, a keen ear and observation, and the ability to present that singular character within the group are needed. Your character should not talk like the group but like an individual. Contrary to the song, not every American speaker says 'tom-ay-to' (as opposed to the English 'tom-ah-to'). In fact, in General American dialect, there are three variant ways of saying tomato. We have all heard criticisms of inaccurate American accents in radio plays.

A script may offer you what looks like a 'pure' dialect initially but no living speaker, and no character who avoids stereotyping, speaks in a 'pure' dialect. The playwright and director quite rightly can demand a more uniform and representative dialect and that can be part of the listener's pleasure in a 'dialect play'. We feel affection, even sentimentality, for some local dialects, along with curiosity, and they preserve a disappearing subculture. There are classics of literature written in dialect, like Mark Twain's *Huckleberry Finn* and Burns's poems in Lowland Scots. But dialect can also mean the languages of the newest emerging subgroups, especially among the young who constantly manufacture new speech, such as rap and freshly-coined crossovers in second- and third-generation ethnic groups.

How heavily you lay on the dialect is always a matter of balancing the style and demands of the play, as well as how you answer the key questions for your character (see Chapter 7). Of course you may be presented with the most direct dialect choice in a cameo role, as a waiter or a passerby, or as a villain, say, in comedy. That solves your problem once you are believable.

If the story is set in today's time, you search for markers – key words and expressions – which help the listener know precisely who you are. Some of the clues are on the page. For example, your character is the sort who says, 'lounge', 'sitting room' or 'parlour'. It could be your vocal habits and word selection that are not socially acceptable or, alternatively, put you into the 'overclass'. It could also include the way you use inbreaths and outbreaths, and pauses. Your dialect choices are part of what creates that single character at those given times in given places in the play scenes.

Whatever your choices, you must be accurate, though not mechanical. An exacting actor's dialect exercise is to voice the different ways the word 'man' is said across the United Kingdom and Ireland, and then across the USA. Try, again as spoken across the UK, the words: 'laugh', 'bath', 'grass', 'dance', 'night', 'cup', 'love' and 'flood'. And then, 'a better bit of butter'. This brings us to the dangers of the glottal stop in Cockney, where the final 't' becomes a glottal stop before another word beginning with a vowel. So we have, 'a better bi- [glottal stop] of butter'. Some speakers use the glottal stop before all vowels, whether or not there is a word boundary, so saying 'a be- [glottal stop] -er bi- [glottal stop] of bu- [glottal stop] -er'. This is technically termed the simpler glottal stop, as it is applied much more widely in speech, and it is notoriously on the march in Estuary English dialect, the mix of popular-London-cum-Cockney spoken around the Thames estuary and beyond. If your choice is the simpler glottal stop, using it on all occasions where 't' comes before a vowel, that may well suit. But you have to create a convincing 'naturalness', and avoid sounding slurred with over-intrusive use of it. Just be warned off by the overuse of the simpler glottal stop in *EastEnders*.

Dialects are always changing and no one speaker in real life conforms to the group norm. That is why I have discussed dialect after other features of the voice, because stress, pitch, breathing and how words join together (juncture) are all part of dialect and talk. Fiction dialogue needs to exaggerate the differences between characters and often makes a speaker more typical of his or her dialect. Again to use the technical language of those who study dialect, dialectologists, a character in a radio play most often conforms to the group norm and 'scores' highly within a dialect, showing least variation. Radio drama lives in distinct dialect boundaries and for the best of reasons. To many listeners, dialect means home.

So dialect faces the actor with the sum total of what language is. It is about pronunciation, the voice stream, grammar, meaning and vocabulary, and about class, gender, politics and geography, the passing of time, and even religion. A character's dialect is the result of the choices available within the script and you hope that the playwright serves you well. If you are cast in a contemporary play, you use your observation skills and experience. Actors are always keen to extend their dialect range and you may be able to add to the list in your *c.v.*

But you could be on Mars in a sci-fi, or be a flowering plant, or a medieval heretic in southern France, or a Puritan farmer. You often have to do some research, and you certainly use your imagination, or you depend on your director's notes or on what passes for fictional dialects of these times and situations. It is often said that people in the Appalachian region of the United States 'speak pure Elizabethan English'. Since they did not get there until 200 years after the death of Shakespeare's Elizabeth, and no dialect is preserved unchanged, it can only be some features of pronunciation and grammar that have been retained as relics. But your listeners are not to know that and you can 'cheat' as it is termed. What matters is what convinces the listeners and you could become a convincing Appalachian farmer of the 1700s with a good sprinkle of 'Shakespeare'.

What matters, in total, is that your dialect work on the final tape sounds accurate and effortless, and does not give the impression that you have had to concentrate on it. You will find the dialect embedded in the rhythms, word order and vocabulary of the script. Often the dialect is the key to the whole role, especially if in a 'dialect' or regional play, though it must not sound as if it has been added-on. You must not sound like the 'stage Irish person' or 'stage Scots person'. Practising over and over again to get up a new dialect is like drill work for the actor. You can test your fluency by improvizing and getting in touch with your feelings in it.

But dialect is only part of your voice and speech work and that is why you must take the holistic approach. It combines with the other aspects of the voice described in this chapter: pitch, volume, breathing, tempo and voice qualities. All of these flow together into the character's voice stream. It is through this holistic approach that you will find the 'centre' to your character's voice, in its placement (using the front of the mouth more, or resonating in the nose or throat), pitch (what notes are sounded the most) and its uniqueness.

Check list: dialect

Be accurate in dialect but don't be too 'pure' or 'stagey'.
Be the individual character not the group.
Be holistic, combine dialect with speech and voice work.

Director John Taylor says, 'I discuss accent and diction from the beginning. They both can be sloppy early on in the production process.' Hilary Norrish reinforces this. 'Choosing accents and regional accents is a deeply political act on radio. You can't undercut it or move it left of field – it's central to the direction. Say you have a man who beats his wife and goes to the pub; well, 99% of radio productions seem to give him a northern accent. On TV, the same guy will have a flash suit and they'll undercut it in some way. Sailors always seem to be from Bristol. I will not cast stupid, rustic Mummerset. The danger on radio is that we stereotype. But most actors are available, from all over the country; no matter where they live, they have a London booking, they travel.'

Letters page, *Radio Times*, 17 January 1947
The domestic servant is rarely a sniffing, giggling, timid half-wit. On the other hand, she has rarely attained a cultured or even correct accent free from local colour. Please don't permit so many plays to lose atmosphere through inept characterisation of domestics.
James Dixon, Cheadle Hulme.

Your voice doctor for radio

Liane Aukin, director:
Vocal defects can be irritating, and they can also give quality and interest. But as for the 'vocally challenged'! – don't cast a stutterer for a start. These features become defects in actors whose performances you are not enjoying and then they come over, you notice them. Any actor must work on a fault, the more control they have the better. But so long as they think and feel correctly, a fault can become memorable.

Here are the problems that need the 'voice doctor':

Eccentric vocal setting: each actor's is unique – having false teeth, for example.

Sibilancy: Too much use of 's' and 'sshh', through gaps in teeth, and lisping. Sibilancy is the overforcing of the 's' sound and there can be danger phrases in the script. The actor who is prone to this problem must keep the 'ss' down because they come over harshly on broadcast. Directors note even more 'ss' in young actors in recent years, due to dialect changes such as Estuary English and to fashion, and they describe it as unattractive and intrusive. The solution should be to move slightly away from the microphone or to speak across it, but if there is a structural problem, the actor cannot avoid overuse of the 's'. Liane Aukin explains, 'The sibilant "s" becomes distorted and exaggerated on the microphone. For the director, the only solution is to edit – you just slice it out and it takes an awful lot of time on analogue tape, nobody wants to do it. A good editor is skilled to push the tape backwards and forwards on the tape head. You could drive yourself crazy doing it and the process is breath-taking.'

Rhotacization: An imperfect 'r' sounded as 'w' (the 'wuh'). It is not always unattractive.

Problems with consonants: especially 'd' and 't' and a failure to articulate clearly. Spot the difficult words in a script, such as 'statistics', 'suspect', 'probably'.

Poor dialect work: such as inaccuracy with the region and problems with the correct pitch patterns needed.

Odd rhythms and inflections.

Intrusive reactions: which come over as unwelcome when voiced during another character's lines.

Colds, huskiness and excessive nasality, and voice fatigue. Also the mouth can be too dry or too wet. Liane Aukin comments, 'The main problem is to avoid sniffing a lot and coughing. A head cold gives the voice an interesting timbre or it's gravelly. A cold is more likely to affect stamina and the actor has to fight it harder on the level of concentration.'

Labial clicks or lip-popping. Liane Aukin again: 'I've never come across a compulsive lip-smacker and usually, once the actor has been told, it's got under control. Like all these features, it can be of use. When I directed *Anna Karenina,* a character in the novel has a facial twitch which irritates, and the actor invented a wonderful equivalent, a vocal twitch.'

Gaps and slowness in pace and tempi.

Intrusive paralanguage: especially gasps and heavy breathing. This is a matter for the director to spot and correct. Liane Aukin continues about breathing, 'It's part of the process after all, because there is a breath at the beginning of every sentence and normally this is not picked up by the microphone. Noisy inhaling and exhaling is surprisingly rare, but every so often either you or your editor call out, "that's a breath" and out it goes.'

Poor volume control, popping and blasting.

These problems are remediable, but imperfect vocal mechanism is not. What I mean is a voice machine that is running down badly, like an actor with poorly-fitting false teeth. Liane Aukin tells of an actor who had to play an old man with obvious gums, 'and to our horror, he whipped out his teeth. I took it as brave and honourable to the profession to play with such artistic integrity, and he had to be begged to put them back in!'

What all this adds up to is that you have to be heard perfectly by the listener, the first time round on broadcast. After all, listening to a radio play is like listening to a real-life conversation in some ways and that is partly the reason why radio is a friend to so many. When we process a stream of speech, we analyse the sound waves, split it up into words and identify the meaning of the words. Somehow we disassemble and reassemble all this continuously, and in real life, even in the middle of a noisy party. This is called the 'cocktail party effect', where the human ear can pick out a speaker from the hubbub all around in a way a microphone cannot.

A scientific study of how people recognize words discovered that the beginnings and endings are more important than the middles. This is called the 'bathtub effect', as if the word is like someone lying in a bath, with their head out of the water at one end and their feet at the other. Remember each word's 'bathtub' and the greater likelihood of not being understood if you slur the beginning or the end of a word. Vowels are heard more easily than consonants, especially stressed vowels.

Relaxation

Training gears the actor up to stay both relaxed and ready at the same time. This does not come easily or quickly. In the American Method, for example, the student actor only attains efficient control after three or four years of daily exercise, according to Lorraine Hull, the author of *Strasberg's Method*, about Lee Strasberg in the Actors Studio. Relaxation technique allows you to be more creative and more open to feeling. You become better able to take in the detail of a director's instructions and to give out in your performance. The key to vocal control is through the whole body mechanism for muscular relaxation. In voice training, your first question is, 'Where does the voice start?' The answer is, the whole body, and especially your spine, finding your centre and balance, and then working on the bellows mechanism itself.

One of Stanislavski's first discoveries was that relaxation and stage creativity go together. His follower Michael Chekhov, nephew of the playwright, went further and instructed his students in what he termed the Feeling of Ease. This got around the conscious process within the actor's mind to a more immediate physical result. Once you have worked on your energy channels, particularly along your spine, your diaphragm and your centre, you are then ready to concentrate on directing that energy through to your vocalization. You must know how to balance yourself and to distribute your weight. Whatever training you continue with as a working actor, relaxation and concentration exercises must be adapted to working days in a radio studio.

Tension is the danger. It makes the actor less precise, closes down the thinking part of the brain, and causes a fall into cliché. The tense actor is also in danger of making unnecessary and unwanted movements, of becoming a script rustler and of straying from the mark around the microphone. You also transmit that tension to other members of the cast and they won't thank you for it. Worst of all, tension first shows itself in the voice as your breathing gets shallower and your pitch notes go up higher, due to your larynx not being relaxed. As your chest, mouth and throat muscles constrict, you produce less resonance. There is simply not enough opening out for your resonating mechanism to work as you want. Relaxation and concentration go together, and relaxation exercises make you more confident and – ask a working actor – more intelligent. A quick tip is to relax with a laugh. Controlled deep breathing is the best way to reducing stress.

As you have to spend so much time on your feet at the microphone, you must know the optimal stance for your feet and how to shift weight. You must be able to move easily from the waist for turns. In the radio studio you do not have to do 'rubber-necking', the leaning into frame of TV and film, but you have to be in complete control of your moves and head shifts. Because the radio actor has to switch from rehearsal to performance and back again, so often and so swiftly, muscular and vocal tension are even more of a danger. So round the radio studio you often see actors stretching and bending, doing crosswords or knitting. Pam Brighton warns, 'If you're experienced and confident as a director, the actors do not pick up on your tension.' While for Angela Pleasence, 'one of the most remarkable things about radio is the complete relaxation. You don't have to learn the lines – it's like doing exams, learning lines. I do a wonderful play on radio all day, and come home and relax. I go dancing down Regent Street to the BBC.'

Relax – to be energetic, ready and quick-thinking

Get your energy flow going and channel it to your mouth and head.
Centre yourself and keep a flexible spine.
Keep on with your relaxation exercises in the studio and outside.

Actors and energy

Kerry Shale:
One of the most difficult things is conserving your energy. Sometimes you've all done what everybody in the studio considers a brilliant take, but for technical reasons, it needs to be done again. Then another actor makes more than a one-word fluff, more than something that can be repaired with a small insert – he approaches it in another way, and that needs another take. And then you're on your fourth or fifth take, and it becomes difficult. You get lost. It's also a temptation to disperse energy in the green room. Radio plays are generally really good fun and only occasionally have I done one I didn't enjoy. With a big group of actors gossiping in the green room between takes (and even in the studio during a take), energy gets wasted. Then you come into the studio too tired to give a good performance. I get energized by the studio. Talking, having fun, is one of my biggest faults.

Jilly Bond:
After three days in the RDC [Radio Drama Company], I had a terrible backache. I was advised to 'sit down whenever you have a break between takes.' And that worked. Sitting in the green room, not knowing just when they'll call you, although there is a schedule, is a problem and adds to tension in the neck and shoulders, always something actors are prone to.

What you can do

Record a radio play scene off air and listen to it. Listen more than once, identifying each of the five aspects of the voice from this chapter. Keep listening across the radio dial. Try the same exercise on real voices on radio: on radio phone-ins (including local radio) and on actuality clips (short quotes from people on the news).

Continue observation of voice from real-life talk. As an exercise, close your eyes occasionally and listen. Try this where you can hear people talk, as on a bus, in a café, on TV, or among friends. When you hear a voice on the phone, identify its five aspects and its voice stream. What are the special markers of each voice you hear? Check out the imperfections and pin each of these down. Real-life talk is full of imperfections because it does not need perfect performance to function and to give meaning.

Get expert training for your voice: with daily exercises and use manuals like Morrison, *Clear Speech*. See the Reading List.

Don't become a 'radio clone'!: Avoid the danger of clustering by having techniques ready to transform your character's voice speedily, as the director needs. These changes include dialect, age, socio-economic status, habitual pitch, pitch patterns and paralanguage. Listen to characters in *The Archers,* especially the women, for examples of how to solve clustering problems.

Study a character from a TV soap: Choose one with a voice range nearest to what you can offer. Identify his or her markers, especially voice qualities (such as huskiness, breathiness, squeakiness). For closer study, record an episode and listen to it with the vision turned off so you can concentrate on a scene or two. Be warned! More than one character in an English soap needs the voice doctor. Now study characters in *The Archers* where you can observe lots of excellent radio technique.

Chapter 7

Putting it all to work

Some actors find it difficult to get down to work on a radio script because it means engaging right off with the product, or performance. Coming from the stage process, they need to find the voice, to get it free and to get the thinking behind the character, before the script will come out right. But with radio, you have to be totally committed to the part from the moment you start your study on it. This still leaves room for exploring, for rehearsal decisions and to be instinctive. In this chapter, I bring together all that has been discussed so far, get it all working for you, and suggest how to unblock difficulties.

PREPARATION AND 'KEEPING IN'

By the time you stand to the microphone for the first scene in the day's schedule, waiting for the cue light, you may have been through one or more well-known techniques of preparation. These serve your concentration and to 'keep you in'. For many actors, it is enough to have done their homework and the read-through, taken director's notes and marked up their script. After all, in the unique situation of acting to the script, no further preparation may be needed. A glance at the top of the scene and down the pages gives the answers to, for example, the key questions that I will outline (see page 119). But that already accomplishes a main part of preparation. Whatever you do, you need techniques to help you lift the text off the page, and to find and retain the truth of the character.

Try these four preparation techniques

Ask the key questions.
Use sensory imagination (creating the place).

Find key words and a physical action (psychological gesture).

Preparation by character and emotion.

All these are in keeping with the through-line of the character and your objectives in the scene. You use these in combination, picking what suits each scene. Of course, actors use other techniques. Nothing beats studying your role right through the play.

Preparation has already been discussed in terms of voice and body relaxation in the previous chapter. Again, as throughout this book, I presume that you are building on stage preparation techniques for centering yourself, for getting into role, and that you can work on character's biography, and on concentration. My task is to select what suits studio work, where preparation is fast and a whole play can be recorded in a day, and to provide you with an expanding resource for your career. You have to prepare for, say, a thirty-minute play of fifteen scenes in total, an hour-and-a-half play of as many as thirty-five scenes, and these scenes are split into sequences for recording purposes. There is not time for improvisation as in the rehearsal room or in training; or for Method techniques, such as speaking out as the character, emotional recall and working on prior events, or Lee Strasberg's 'taking a moment'. Though of course there is the model of the English 'cool' actor, as Angela Pleasence explains of herself, 'I can't become involved with getting into character. If I could, I'd stand on my head and twiddle my foot, but I have to go zoom! Straight into it! Otherwise, I'd have dissipated my energies earlier.'

Let me go to Stanislavski for some terms long established in theatre. You have already made your choices about your character and voice, in your study. These have been according to the given circumstances of the play, as you discovered them. Not all choices are equally valid and once you get into the studio, you bring them into line with the objectives set by the director in the read-through. So choices become the decided objectives and all are determined by the overall shape of the play, the superobjective. An objective in a scene can be redecided, that is what a lot of rehearsal is about, and further choices examined. You contribute to the discussion by offering your choices. The new decision is an adjustment. So the rehearsal process is: choices become objectives, which can be changed by adjustments into new objectives, and all in line with the superobjective of the play.

If you are working on 'rehearse-record', you constantly shift from recording the finished sequence or scene, and back into rehearsal mode of choices and objectives. The danger here is that you might want to make a later adjustment to your character and voice to suit the play that is emerging or because you have met a block. But the initial groundwork is final, once in the can. You must hold to the character's voice that was the original agreed objective, as part has already been recorded. So you have to go to other techniques to unblock yourself.

You meet problems. These could emerge as a feeling that you are not concentrating and relaxing correctly for the microphone, or that you are rushing or slowing the pace, or not listening and staying in. You could feel you are no longer fully in character and you miss detail and moments. The recording system of 'at-a-run' gives you more time, progressively to build your character. But no matter what system you work by, once you meet a block, try the following four techniques of preparation. You will not have the freedom to unblock by trying out a radically different choice for your character, as in the stage rehearsal room. But radio technique will free you and improve your concentration, and release new energy to carry you through the scene. The hard fact is that in radio, as in the film medium, you have fewer choices once production has begun. You may have to stick to an objective you do not favour. Director Jeremy Mortimer makes some use of improvisation. 'I give the actors the first and last lines of a scene, and I record all they do. Rehearsal is potentially the most deadening part of the process. Improvisation creates a different sort of sound to the averagely-scripted play – some listeners find it confusing but others find it truer to life.'

Key questions

'Where am I?' and 'What has brought me to this point?'

'What obstacles will I meet?'

Let us begin with the key questions. At the beginning of each scene, ask yourself as a character: 'Why am I here and where am I?', 'What has brought me to this point?', 'How do I feel about the other people in this scene?' and 'What obstacles will I meet?' Think through your objective in the scene, your character's action, and how far you will go to get what you want. Run over these questions rapidly in your mind. It will help you to concentrate, and your answers will help you to decide whether to go on to more preparation. Your grasp of the overall script is essential from study and the read-through, and you should mark up your script in your own way as shorthand. A particular squiggle could be the rapid answer, meaning 'my partner thinks I'm guilty again', or a significant clue to a crime in a thriller that recurs through the play. You will find ways of marking up your script in the appendix.

'Where am I?'

'Where am I?' is crucial and takes you on to the next technique: creating the place by sensory imagination. You could be on Venus or a night bus, in a freezing bed, in a chocolate castle or a kitchen. As you are on the stage of the microphone where there is nothing of the scenery in front of you, only the set and Spot's materials, you must use your actor's imagination as in no other medium. You may handle no props and see no object that you can endow with emotion and meaning, least of all a costume, as Stanislavski and others advise for the stage. You do not have the play's environment to inhabit, to 'make it real'. You have to rouse your imaginary senses to create the scene's location and to inhabit it.

All depends on your ability to respond to fictional stimuli and to select for radio's needs; and whether your actor's pathway is to make it real for yourself as both actor and character crossing over with each other, or whether you work within a boundary of the character as a created fiction. To explain this basic contrast further: some actors make it real (Stanislavski and/or Method trained) and some make it convincing (the 'technique' or 'cool' actor, the traditionally-viewed English actor as opposed to the American). Real objects in a set can help to induce belief and concentration, but all actors have to work from imaginary, non-material objects, relationships and situations.

Remember that you are working in parallel with the listeners, the 'final actor', who have to create the 'second play' in their minds, using their sensory imagination. They cannot make it live for themselves unless you have concentrated your senses into your acting. Jane Morgan explains, 'I always get my actors to imagine the scene they've come from, to think "What was I doing before?". You always have to be doing something – needlework, making a cake? – because you can't just say the lines standing in front of the microphone.'

Five senses

Explore your five senses: sight, touch, smell, taste and hearing.

Look for the sensory trigger.

Here are a few of the many techniques used to rouse the actor's imagination to work on the scene. Again, I rely on your previous training work on the five senses. First you must look for the sensory trigger in the scene. It could be a single one, like the smell of cooking in the kitchen or the cold touch of the bed. Or the sci-fi Venus could be a combined experience of rainbows and sulphurous atmosphere, sight, taste and smell. In the night bus you are tired and the experience is mainly one of sound, shouts and engine.

In your study, run through your five senses to test out each scene, bringing them in, one at a time. Now select, according to the given circumstances and your character's objective. This will help when you return to the kitchen location, for example, in another scene. Fill in more of your character's life, as the playwright has only given you a slice of it and there are many gaps. What does your character cook? The smell, taste and sight of it and its ingredients will hang around the kitchen. Thinking 'beans' or 'egg' or 'tuna' could be your trigger. This will also be useful if later in the day your director needs a quick retake because some technical hitch has surfaced.

Another trigger is your own fantasy. A lot of your acting material is what you have not actually experienced yourself, however many parallels on which you can draw. Make the most of a rich fantasy life and you might live the life of, and dream the dreams of, your character for a short while. Radio being the blind medium, the sense that calls on your imagination most is sight. Since listeners talk about the best pictures being on radio, they depend on your powers of visualization. Of course the playwright should already have done a lot of the work, often by the power of the situations and detailed description embedded in the dialogue.

Creative visualization will fill the situation and place for you. As you guide yourself through the environment, check each of the five senses and make your efficient selection. Visualizing uses more than sight to make it 'real'. It also uses touch, smell, hearing and taste. Do not turn it into a dream but ground yourself in the given circumstances of the scene, in your objective and the obstacles you face. You visualize with the 'inner eye' and you have to train yourself to do this in your studio preparation keeping your eyes open. This is a particular requirement if you work in the dead room which is smaller and enclosed and needed for outside scenes. Nothing more starkly exhibits how acting on radio is unique in itself than when the actor comes to apply training exercises in visualization and 'objects of attention' to the blind medium. These stage exercises move from working with the real object (food, sunshine, mirror, clothes) and then creating the reality without the object, and alternating between them.

For the Stanislavskian actor on stage, concentration means having an object of attention, real or imaginary, for every moment. Your radio focus has to be on objects and situations solely imaginary, through more selective techniques. Radio's compensation is that you are not directly the object of attention yourself in the studio; you are not required to be 'private in public' as a performer must be on stage or in front of the film crew. All your energy can flow into your acting to the microphone and relating to your dialogue partners.

Key words and actions

Use a phrase or key word or sound as a trigger.

A key physical or psychological gesture can lead to the feeling.

Use your muscle groups to stimulate the feeling.

Another technique of preparation is to use key words, saying them to yourself quietly or silently before the cue light goes on. They could be a phrase from the script which sums up the objective or the obstacle for your character in the scene, or a triggering emotion, not as such from the script. The key could be reduced to one word or a sound linked to a key emotion. A key word or sound is particularly suited to radio.

The key stimulus could also be a physical action, evocative and wordless. It has to be something possible in the limits of the studio and as you stand ready or as you move. Your character could have just come down the stairs or from a car, a spaceship or a hackney coach. There could be a key action in the scene, like a slap (threatened or carried out), crushing a letter or holding a gun. You can go into your cue, if possible, by evoking some of that activity. You can also awake the muscular memory and emotion in yourself by flexing the muscle group needed to carry out your 'movements'. All this can help to colour and detail your performance. If you make an approach, such as a move from position 5, you are fortunate to have preparation there for you, but many cues are from a static position where you are at your mark.

This physical action has a long history in twentieth-century theatre. Michael Chekhov, nephew of the playwright, suggested the 'psychological gesture', abbreviated to PG, as preparation. 'You look for a suitable all-over gesture which can express all this in the character.' A wilful domineering character, for example, thrusts his arm downward and outward, while the rest of his body recoils upward and back away from it. 'The qualities which fill and permeate each muscle of the entire body, will provoke within you feelings of hatred and disgust, you penetrate and stimulate the depths of your own psychology.' The action leads to the feeling. So you can invent your radio PGs, especially using muscle groups linked to feeling and with your spare arm, clenching, shaking, waving and loosening. Facial expression dramatically alters the voice, so smile, screw up your nose, rub your eye, wink. Get that look in your voice! You must find the situation and the feeling, and do not wait to let them find you. Though Tessa Worsley finds, 'I don't have time to trigger before a take. I just concentrate for those few moments. It's very hard always to be truthful.'

Preparation by character and emotion

Radio is selective about voice. You have to look to its short cuts, or to its shorthand. Follow all the clues about your character to get as directly as you can to the voice and find your character's journey through the play. You may have to make notes about what has happened before the play script begins, the pre-text life of your character. Some characters are described in more detail in the radio script, or they are stock characters, stereotyped perhaps by the play's genre. Creating the radio version of an adapted stage play may give you more clues because there are often more personality and appearance clues from which to work. Finding the voice does not serve the whole purpose of the character and that is why I have stressed 'body language'. Radio is the one medium where you never have to play yourself, for the stage actor must always bring something of themselves to the audience. Radio allows a split between the actor and the character. All actors construct 'masks.' Some of these are protective or arise from the demands of the role, and others allow freer expression.

To get into the radio character, you find the voice and dialect speedily. More often you get to 'see' the character and build up their world. You discover appearance from age, gender, clothing, socio-economic grouping, personal geography, culture, temperament and outlook, movement and from your character's nearest and dearest. Building the character is such a basic of acting that I do not have to add to the many useful guides that exist. What you have to work on in detail is your character's voice: vocabulary, rhythms, qualities and dialect as I outlined in the previous chapter. A person lives in their voice just as they live in their world, for voice is the centre of the 'psychophysical', body and mind. Make your voice wear your character's clothes and move as they do, and share their health and diet. As an experiment, you might take out all the punctuation from your script – the full stops, commas and dashes – and discover afresh the rhythms of your character. Try this in your study.

Only you can discover individuality, even when you work in 'shorthand' for a smaller stock cameo role: waitress, the destitute, soldier or the third witch. Think of these as wearing a voice 'uniform', probably the most required of them to fit into the whole play. But you can let the listener see the 'face' attached to the uniform. There is a greater challenge on radio in what are called 'extended' characters. These make more demands on emotion, or their voices must fit 'stretched' bodies (fat or thin, chronic pain and illnesses, monsters, ageing, being ugly and stigmatized). It is difficult to cough fluently in character, as someone living with AIDS or enfeebled with the Black Death. Radio can cope with ageing perhaps better than the make-up department and when you extend yourself from youth into old age in a 'biog' play, think through the 'voice core' and how the vocal chords age.

A scene with peak emotions, such as anger, love and shock, often demands a swifter pacing on radio than in any other medium. You are left with so little space to work outside the words themselves and you cannot explore the subtext of the face as in other media where the camera and stage would allow reactions and a slower development. The build to the peak, the peak itself and the aftershock can be over so fast, relatively, that it leaves you with little space for preparation. You have to trust to the script. There is both a stretching and a shrinking here; a stretching of the words so they bear their full weight and a shrinking of the gaps between them.

STAYING IN AND KEEPING CONNECTED

Having covered preparation and beyond, I now want to consider staying in, or how to keep connected with your scene partners and the audience. Getting in touch, and keeping in touch with other actors, and through them and the microphone to the listeners, is the essential of radio acting. A problem is that what Stanislavski summarized as communication depends on direct contact with the stage spectator, or in the indirect medium of film, with the camera. The transferring of thoughts, words and emotions is from stage actor to partner to audience.

The radio actor's voice and connecting mechanism, including eyeline, are firstly from script to microphone, and only secondly from actor to actor, and then only if the sound set, blocking and technique allow. Stanislavski took communication further, to subtext and even 'radiation of Prana rays', for him the most intense form of creative message-giving. You must bring yourself to feel that there are listeners on the receiving end, even when the style of the play is 'fourth wall', a realism where the microphone is an eavesdropper. You must make that connection whether you think of acting to an ideal and individual listener, or to listeners in general who are attentive and sympathetic. What you must avoid is breaking the bond, the feeling that there is nobody on the receiving end, and you are sealed off in the studio.

The first connection is with the other actors in the play and here techniques from stage training must be directly useful. You'll know when things go wrong because you will feel the energy flagging between you, you are not being listened to and you are now left apparently talking to yourself. Or the dialogue has become too much of a ping-pong, that you are not 'staying in'. The pace gets out of sync, and you either dawdle or you rush, or you get the emphasis wrong and lose detail, and slur. The fault could also be that you are concentrating on getting it right to the person who means most to you – that is yourself – with that voice inside intrusively giving you instructions, the 'me' actor talking to the 'I' character and taking over. But whatever, you realize you have broken the connection. The first solution is to go back to your preparation. Try a trigger through your five senses (getting the smell of the place) or a key word or question ('Where am I?') to 'make it real' for you, to get the 'on-microphone' reality, like the on-stage reality. Try a quick bit of relaxation.

Substitution

This means substituting for the actor in front of you an image of another who more nearly resembles the character for you. In Method, this is called personalization, and the substitute created has a personal meaning for the actor and comes from their own lived experience. So in a love scene, you could superimpose the imaginary features of a lover, or in a family situation, your own parents. Radio substitution can mean creating all or some of the details of the other character and imaginatively seeing that character with you in the studio. It depends on the degree of visualization you find yourself using in the play both for locations and characters, on how specific the script is in its descriptions and on the style of the play, such as a thriller or comedy or historical drama. It may come all the clearer if your script is an adaptation of a stage play and you can see the stage action and scenery in your mind's eye.

Since, as I have said earlier, visualization is the task of the receiving listeners, it is necessary that all involved in the production construct their own sound pictures. Indeed, you hear frequent discussion of the sound pictures, checking their detail is appropriate in building the sound sets and that they have their own consistent logic. It could be that your partners resemble their role, in which case you can use a sort of substitution. If not, especially as this is radio, then try a stronger substitution technique.

Endowing and centre

Rather than full-scale substitution, you can try 'endowing', that is adding to your partner actor some feature or other from the character. Their face might change, or their body and stance, in your imagination. You could try seeing that character in movement, walking distinctively and maybe even with a twitch or repetitive hand gesture.

You can combine that with centre technique. In training, actors work on creating their own centre and then realizing a centre for a character. This is the psychological and balancing centre of the body, and finding the centre is a technique in concentration, and for a character it could be the pivotal point from which all energy is directed and to which it flows. Try finding such a centre for your partner's character and then mentally attach to it a string, as if that was the leading point by which the character could be dragged across an imaginary line. These are standard training exercises and you can translate them at speed in the studio by your imagination. Already you will have picked up a lot of clues about the other characters' inner lives.

Your acting experience informs you that there is a constant to-and-fro of energy in dialogue. You send and receive signals and this operates like a feedback loop, that is, you make immediate adjustments and are reacted to in turn. You make constant balancing changes with your actor partners, in rhythm, emphasis and emotion, feeding off each other. Radio has another advantage in 'looping,' as you can signal to each other unseen to the microphone and the listener. On radio you can be both actor and character.

First entrance

There remains one other technical hurdle to discuss – your first radio 'entrance'. When you first come on, on screen or on stage, the audience makes immediate judgements about you. Indeed, as your character, you send out an energetic mass of visual signals to be read: who you are, what you look like and why you are here, and then you speak your first line. In acting school, you are instructed to 'enter in character', how and when to take up your entrance cue from offstage, and to build your entrance. Mishandle your entrance and you delude your audience. You have to 'step into the character's shoes' and be on, taking up your cue immediately.

Your first lines tell the listener of your character's dialect (age, geography, socio-economic status, gender) and identity. This information could be later adjusted or confirmed, but you have to be sure of these signals when recording because you stick by them. The difference with radio is that the revealing of character must be gradual and progressive, whatever the signalling you do with your first lines. Stage and screen give a complete display of body, costume and face. Again, you will do better with preparation and thinking through your character's journey.

You are the only judge of what works for you from this chapter. Unfortunately, the radio studio is not an easy place for experiment as it is used solely for work. There are no rehearsal rooms or laboratories for radio drama. Above all, be aware of what could work for you and explore it with a tape recorder, and possibly some fellow actors. Do not be forced into a technique; you do not have to use what does not suit you. Do not be burdened by theory about having to find your key words, objective and obstacle. Many actors work intuitively, without having to talk about how they work and you should not carry unnecessary baggage into the studio. But a 'natural' actor can only be creative in the studio with good microphone skills.

THE 'TEN-PLUS' RADIO ACTING STYLES

Gielgud said the first task of the actor is to find the play's style. To give you a rough guide on this, I have identified ten radio drama styles. I have noted what is most typical of radio, and its various 'strands', and the slots in which the plays are broadcast, especially as there are so many new plays and one-shot productions. As with every play, for stage or whatever medium, you look as an actor to period, genre and where the play locates itself along that spectrum from realism to non-realism, and anti-realism (expressionism etc.), and what its cultural references are. We have to map out radio territory here so that even if we are dealing with an adaptation from the stage (Ayckbourn, Shaw, Shakespeare) what matters is the radio treatment it gets and the BBC 'house' styles. The ten styles to look for are: realist or 'standard production', 'classic' acting in repertoire stage plays (adaptations, including classic novels), monologues and interiorizing 'thoughts', narrator, comedy, Children's Theatre (Radio 4), genre (especially thriller, horror and sci-fi), soap, regional (dialect and production outside London) and finally, non-realist.

The mainstream of radio drama is realist and I coin the term 'standard production' for this. It is a complete production-package for director, Spot and cubicle, who well understand the conventions, and who can work speedily on each new play. Changing from it can make production slower, whether on location or to suit the needs of an experimental director, working perhaps with improvisation. With its nearly seventy-five year history, I think of the BBC as the Hollywood of radio plays. Just as we refer to the 'classical narrative cinema' of Hollywood from the 1940s up to the early 1960s, so most plays bear proudly the stamp of 'BBC'. These are achievements and a tradition that have never received full credit. In 'standard production' there is:

Strict foreground/background in perspective. The voices are mixed and balanced so that they stand out prominently from the atmos or sound background, rather than being embedded in it like dialogue in many film sound tracks. Crowd scenes are built like this to avoid confusion for the listener. The actor's voice is balanced against the atmos rather than the sound background creating a 'habitat' for the voice.

Sound picture and its perspective. These are organized strictly around a 'sound centre' that remains fixed centrally. Less often does the production follow the characters 'up the garden path', so to speak, with a moving sound centre. See Chapter 4 about how to 'travel on the line' and the note in the script 'we go with'.

'Standard-production' realism is much plainer. The neutral acoustic (narrator's mike, interiorizing), or near-neutral acoustic (living room), is common. This throws the interest on to the voices. The favourite microphone position is 3 (conversation). Sometimes a director uses a more filmic style with a lot more detail in the sound picture, with some interest in the middle ground (between foreground voices and background atmos).

The style can also be a more edgy and raw actuality, often in thrillers and semi-documentaries, and those with a real-life taste of actuality recording from the newsroom. These variations make different demands on the actors. At the other end of the spectrum is the famous 'Archers' realism. It is a survival from mono production as the move-over to stereo only happened in October 1992. It is so traditional that one type of scene ending is termed 'The Archers fade': each scene ends, not with a straight cut, but with 'fade to black'. Director Jeremy Mortimer works excitingly with ways of achieving radio realisms. 'I find sounding natural on radio is almost like a dialect. Some naturalisms can be very boring or hard to follow, for example, teenagers all talking at once. So I combine it with monologue, which allows the meaning to come forward.'

The second style is 'classic' acting in adaptations of stage plays. There is a production convention that sites the listener in an ideal seat in the stalls, looking into a radio proscenium arch. It more often demands moves and microphone positions 4 and 5. The actor enjoys much more of the 'throw' or projection and volume of voice he or she uses in the theatre. It is the way to do most Shaw dialogue and a lot of Ayckbourn. Shakespeare and English Renaissance theatre will have more variation of positions, because of asides and monologues, realized closer to the microphone. The director can create an exciting sense of the listener being there, in the middle of the radio scene 'stage', surrounded by the characters.

Next comes BBC schools, and the Radio 4 children's play slot, once more extensively served by Radio 5, and it features series like *The Adventures of Tintin*. Acoustics can be much more interesting, with more moves, and thriller adventures create more of a 'habitat' sound background. The most exciting and detailed production can often be found in genre plays, for example the extraordinary *Dracula* adaptation from director Hamish Wilson in Edinburgh.

Less is more

At times you have to pull your performance right down, even to become the 'do nothing' actor, in the positive sense. This applies particularly to radio where the rule is often 'less is more'. You know that for your character, at some points, nothing needs to happen. But when the focus of the scene is away from you it does not mean you fall out of the dialogue. I have discussed how to deal with longish gaps in your lines by adding a reaction (breathing, and 'umms'). But often this is too fussy and not needed. The rule for the 'do nothing' actor here is the same for acting in all the media, even if you are not 'seen': keep up concentration. On stage, a movement that does not fit in, or relaxing or tensing muscles too much, alerts the audience to your lack of concentration.

The other half of the choice (or necessity) of being a 'do-nothing' actor is that you stay 'in' the dialogue. You are not on display before the camera or on stage, but you must send signals to the others that you are in the flow of the dialogue. Your acting is not stop-go and you must be able to pick up your cues with speed and commitment. Another solution is to take a step or two back from your micro-phone position, further out of the microphone field, and out of immediate visual communication with the other actors. Provided this is done noiselessly, it is often the best solution and you can check with the director.

Radio demands less, but you have to keep radiating as Stanislavski called it. Hitchcock was mocking pretentiousness when he described the best screen actor as 'the man who can do nothing extremely well'. Directors I interviewed constantly stressed the need for subtlety of technique, such as Patrick Rayner: 'The young actor's fault is not listening and realizing that the less is the better. What's needed is understatement, not busting every rivet with over-enthusiasm.'

BAD RADIO ACTING AND SOME GREAT SOLUTIONS

Andrew Sachs, actor:
I've given some rotten performances on radio, I'm here to confess. You've got only one day to get into the part and find the role, and you resort to cliché acting.

We all have ideas about bad radio acting. This is not, I insist, because there is much of it about, but because there is a lot of radio drama. Some listeners object to the artificiality of the business in itself. 'When I tune into a radio play, I know what it is instantly, by that way they talk.' I am grateful to actors I interviewed who have been so revealing here. I need to disentangle bad acting from bad production and bad directing. An actor's contract says to 'act as directed', after all and the director could be off-beam. Marlon Brando spoke for the actor's predicament when he said of an early film role of his that it was like 'a rat copulating with a grapefruit'.

A lot on radio can be bettered in the process of post-production editing and mixing. What goes into the microphone need not all come out of the radio speaker and to the listener. Fluffs are cut out and most importantly, pace can be speeded up, though this takes a lot of patient trimming of tape. A bad individual performance can be sliced down, if at all possible. What is a disaster in the studio

might be rescued in editing, to some extent. There are actors' bad
habits which can be edited out, like the intrusive 'umms'. There are
undisciplined actors who add an unscripted 'look' or 'well' as they
take up a cue. Those tiny scraps end up on the editing floor, hopefully. As Matthew Morgan, actor, says, 'It's tiresome. If they do it,
they do it a lot. You get it in actors new to radio and they do it on
stage too. It comes over sounding like a fluff, it's not giving the words
appropriate value.' One director, at some particularly exasperating
retakes, mimed a scissors to me, and murmured, 'I have a very sharp
razor'.

You will hear the truism that bad acting is bad acting no matter
what the medium. Christian Rodska, an actor whose radio work I
greatly admire, said, 'It's like any bad acting. Initially, an actor can
fail on the technical side, but it does not take long to learn, it's just
practice. And it wastes time if an actor has made a technical mistake, when, for example, the director says "you're turning off". But
with some people who have never done radio before, I've thought,
"that's good". While with long-practised actors, I've also thought,
"you haven't got any better".'

Andrew Sachs is refreshingly direct: 'Bad radio acting? – most of
it is! And I include myself. I have given most of my good performances only lately. I'm capable of that now. Mind you, I'd never
start getting better if I thought I was better.' Director Brian Scott-
Hughes says, 'The worst kind is when the actor is totally fluent and
not thinking the lines, it's lacking in spontaneity.' Let us get down to
specifics. For Matthew Morgan, 'the biggest mistake is not acting on
the line'. This is about cue-taking – in leaving a gap before taking up
your cue. It can suddenly drain the energy from that beat of dialogue
and kill the rhythm and flow. Morgan's number two on the list of
gaffes is 'a bad accent which you can't listen to.'

Steve Nallon says, 'You can tell if the lines have just been read,
there's no life, no danger. That's as opposed to being performed.'
Nicola Pagett states, 'It's when actors don't listen to each other.
They're too busy acting and they've decided how to do it. Though
a production depends on everyone being good – otherwise, it won't
be good.'

James Aubrey summarizes: 'With bad actors, you can see them
act. Then there are some actors who are slow at notes and such, and
they are the ones who are slow on stage too. There are people who
don't take it too seriously. Radio can be an easy job, you have to
admit it, this attitude is tempting. You can realize you should have
done some homework to get yourself to the standards of the other
actors or of the director. So actors like that – I call it laziness. It holds

up the rest of the cast and you have to bang that actor over the head and say, "Come on!". Then there's the actor who's pissed after the lunchtime. So no wonder the director has to be a disciplinarian. Bad acting in sum? You don't believe a word they are saying.'

For Kerry Shale, it is 'predictability, and there's a lot of that around. A lot of listeners find it comforting, but when I'm listening, that puts me right to sleep. It's not bad acting, it's comfortable and unadventurous, and it's because the scripts are that. I'm definitely in a minority here, it's a matter of personal taste. I try to find a way round it, if I'm in it, I try to give a bit of reality by underplaying – taking a cliché and trying to humanize it. Here's an example. I was playing a brash Texan once, the sort in a check suit, and the director gave me a note on the talkback, "to overplay", and I said, "What you really want is a cliché?". His reply was, "Yes, that's exactly it." That was his choice, not mine. But I rarely hear bad acting.'

Here now are some directors' views. First, Patrick Rayner. 'Bad acting can crop up in all productions, because of hurry, because the writing needs tricks to make it work and instead you get a house style, a laziness. It's less true of regional productions than metropolitan. I've done it and been party to it, because of hurry. Some actors put on a "radio drama" voice, they confuse radio drama with funny voices. Bad acting is going for the superficial effect. An actor can be clever enough to inflect every word to give a surface reading, but it's not centred. It's performed, but without truth or reality. An actor can have tricks to throw his voice up through the nose and back over his shoulders!' Pam Brighton finds, 'It's about disconnecting – from the scene and from others, as on stage and film. There's also young directors who go into radio without stage experience and where we all get our knowledge of acting is theatre.'

Jonathan James-Moore, Head of BBC Radio Light Entertainment deals with the comedy actor. 'There's the actor who can't cope with the comic pace, he gets stuck on the page. His performance gets to be a series of lines being read, with gaps in between. It depends on acting experience to solve this as it's a difficult problem. It makes editing – cross-cutting – a pain because that sort of actor can get worse with further takes, even to individual lines.' For Lissa Evans, who has worked in the same department and is now an independent, bad acting is, 'actors who don't gauge the mood of a production, or who just don't get it. Or who lose the rhythm of it in front of the audience. Or who just don't get the rhythm of how it's played. Then there are actors who don't listen to how the others are doing things. Some have no timing, and timing is even more important on radio, where there is no distraction. Then there are people with no subtlety in their voice.' The horror for the director is to realize a particular casting mistake while the show is being recorded in front of a live audience, 'You work out how you can trim it, lop out as much as you can of that actor's lines, how you cut certain scenes. If people are that bad, they're unusable. Maybe their role will be fabulous in the theatre after three weeks. I had one actor who underplayed the role in the read-through, and then when we got into the studio, it almost ground to a halt. I practically had to do handstands.'

Hamish Wilson condemns the attitude, "because I don't have to learn it, I can just open the envelope when I walk in the door". He says, 'the message is: you've got to prepare, you've got to know it.'

There is also the difficulty of small or 'cameo' parts. Here is John Taylor who worked on Radio 5 drama. 'Some RDC performances can be dreadful, even though they're skilled actors. It's cameo parts. The problem is that they possess no context for acting them. They come into the production only for one morning which does not give them the time to pick up the little clues and signals that make the unique cameo character. So they deliver a standard performance. Or worse, you get coarse acting. It emerges as sounds stuck on to the play. That's partly our system in the BBC. But some actors can pick up the part, even if small, and get the style.' Jilly Bond's solution is to create a world for the character and to research the lady's maid, for example, 'but if a director wants you to do something that feels a bit boring, then I'm just fodder.'

Then there is the wrong style, explains Gordon House of World Service. 'You get automatic pilot performances. There's the sort of actor who reads the script on the train on his way to the studio. They think, "It's my performance number 3B, the character with the lisp." But then I think it's my fault as a director for not prodding. A lazy director can let it go through on the nod. I don't like the sort of actor with a wonderful voice, the "radio actor's voice". The voice is merely an instrument to realize character. Then you get the actor who has envisaged his performance and you hear that at the read-through and he's done his homework. But you end up with a compromise, neither fish nor fowl. The director has to change his view in the light of what the actor is giving.' For Michael Arditti, radio playwright and theatre critic, previously on the *Evening Standard,* part of the fault is directing. 'It's directors doing two runs and going straight into the take without correcting words even. The actors overdo it, over-emoting, and try to overcompensate for the lack of visuals. I dislike breathy, very throaty acting. The worst acting is all over the place, not controlled, instead of the need for the radio actor to talk mind to mind with the listener. The best?

Anna Massey.' A last problem is the ensemble, for everyone in the studio has to get it right simultaneously. It's no use saying to the director, 'I wasn't good enough, I must have a retake', if others have peaked and it cannot get better.

Problems and solutions

Verbal fluffs and intrusive 'umms'. Master your script. Read all the scenes and be ready to adapt fast and creatively to director's notes.

Not coming in on cue – 'not acting on the line'. Get technical about the studio. Use your spare time to observe the production process if you can. Read more about it. Develop your radio skills.

Emphasizing too many words and putting on an artificial 'radio drama' voice. If you feel you are getting monotonous, stop hitting the same note with the same force each time.

You have not marked up enough on your script. Do it!

WORKING ON A SCRIPT

Choices

Here is the opening of Colin Finbow's *Another Monday,* and I have added notes for you to study the detail of voicing, along with pro- duction. It offers a good plot hook – the situation is that Bob starts his first day as a teacher, having left his previous job in advertising. In the BBC Afternoon Play production, Nicky Henson played the lead, with his husky, deep, 'dark-brown' voice.

> 1. FX: [LAVATORY FLUSH. BATHROOM ATMOS]
> 2. BOB: Murky face of Monday. Me in my best tie and Monday best, unready for a new week. My palms are moist. I can smell my feet.

The actor is at position 2 in a bathroom set, the sound picture is Bob looking at himself in the mirror. This is the hook and the char- acter's entrance, when listeners also read the voice's dialect for the first time. Work out what information is downloaded into the opening and list it. The tight phrases give the actor a lot to work with and it is intriguing in storyline. The big challenge here is tempo. How would you mark the pauses in your script? The echoey atmos and position 2 bring up all aspects of the voice, especially the bass notes, breathing and quality, it makes an intensifying close-up. There is physical description in the script, so use embodying. Allow a pause before FX 3 – it was three seconds in the BBC production. Too much perhaps? Take out all the full stops and commas, all the punctuation in the script and rework it for you.

3. **FX:** SINK PLUG PULLED AND WATER GLUGS OUT

4. **BOB:** Unzip that smile, make a bright new day with Zest. Zest cleans your teeth so white it puts a smile on other people's faces.

The first example of Bob's advertising copy, an indication of his previous job as a 'creative'. It recurs through the storyline. Mood change and role-playing are to be put over. Still in position 2 but with raised volume, switch of head focus and cheerful pitch. Get the embodying in the stretched 'smile' – you make the listener see that Zest smile in Bob's mirror.

5. **JAN:** [calling from below] Darling, your cereal's getting cold.
[Jan is at position five.]

6. **BOB:** Coming darling.

Breaking the reverie, reality coming in, rise in volume, expresses his relationship with his wife. Switch to position 3.

Now make your own notes on the next sequence. There is a straight cut into 7 and the location is the kitchen.

7. **FX:** BREAKFAST, AND NEWS ON RADIO.
RADIO TURNED OFF

8. **JAN:** You look very nice.

9. **BOB:** One does one's best.

10. **JAN:** Don't like the tie though. Bit loud.

11. **BOB:** It's my favourite.

12. **JAN:** Still a bit loud.

13. **BOB:** What's this morning's speciality?

14. **JAN:** Your favourite.

15. **BOB:** Natur-Bran?

16. **JAN:** 'Natur-ally!' Here we go. Milk's hot.

17. **FX:** [SPOT – SPOON ON PLATE]

18. **BOB:** Natur-Bran, delicious hot or cold. Farm fresh flakes of crispy wheat, dusted with sun-ripened sugar and

blended with bran and juicy raisins, to give you a natural start to the day.

19. JAN: You nervous, Bob?

20. BOB: Yes.

21. JAN: You always recite your commercials when you're a bit nervous.

Where would you put in pauses, a sigh or two, and vary the pace? Where is the subtext? Are there any throw-away words or phrases? How would you develop the relationship between the two? What is Spot doing? How do you deal with the advertising copy?

Kevin Day, comedian, on Radio 5:
Have you ever heard a tape of yourself? It's like masturbatin' with your left hand. It's somebody else. It just doesn't sound like you.

Chapter 8

Breaking into the markets

RADIO COMMERCIALS AND VOICE-OVERS

Mandy Wheeler, managing director of Mandy Wheeler Sounds Productions:
'Commercials are sponsored radio dramas, they're drama in one minute.'

When you are called to do a 'voice' in a commercial, it is for:

A character: either single-voice or dialogue.

The single-voice announcement: such as 'If you are over fifty and want car insurance...' Also called the announcer.

Reading an end-line: such as 'Yellow Pages – don't leave home without it'.

Radio commercials are mostly from thirty to sixty seconds and occasionally as long as ninety. There are three ways for actors to work the market. In the first, the top end of the market, you are booked for an hour and you work in the voice booth, which varies in size from so small that you can only sit, to the much larger studio; and of course it is separated from the control room by a glass window. There could be a dozen people in the control room. Along with the producer, writer and technicians, there will be the clients, usually brand managers from the marketing department of the product, and they are all peering through the glass at you. Equity rules allow up to five scripts to be recorded in an hour, but you could be working on only one. This is what is called the 'London circuit', where the fee can be £500 for an hour, plus usage fee for how often the commercial is played. Production studios are usually in Soho.

The second commercials market is mostly in local radio where the bulk of commercials are made and it usually operates by Equity minimum standards. Production time in total for each commercial here is three to five minutes and the fee is £13.50 per commercial and you also earn a session fee for travel into the studio, if you can negotiate it, of between £30 to £50. The station's head of commercial production has to justify the extra fee to the ad agency. You could work on ten to fifteen commercials per session.

The usual recording method for a commercial is to do it once for timing, once for interpretation, once more and then the take.

But the third type of market now predominates for most commercials in many stations. The actor no longer comes into the studio and instead works 'down the line' from his or her own home studio, equipped with mixing desk, sound booth and a special ISDN, a dedicated phone line. This means that the actor has made an investment of some £5,000 for the equipment, plus £1,000 for the dedicated ISDN line, and also the cost of a sound studio.

'Ad' is a term often used but in advertising it is more customary to refer to 'commercial' for radio and TV, and 'ad' for printed matter. The production method for a commercial voice-over (recording your voice in the studio) is the same for both TV and radio. There are two types of voice-over: those for broadcast; and those for 'research' tests for the clients to choose from, and which lead to a final version. There can be five or six actors doing the research tests.

In this corporate environment every second is bought to sell. You will be dealing with 'copy' about products as diverse as insurance and ear-wax remover, that you will make into your script. You are still an actor. You do not have to understand everything about advertising, and who does? There is a famous dictum: 'Everybody knows that half of the money spent on advertising is wasted but nobody knows which half.' So, are you acting or selling? 'If it's apparent you are doing either – you're doing it wrong', says Ralph van Dijk, director and co-founder of Eardrum in London. 'Selling will come through if you believe it. Sound like a real person, not a voice-over.' For Adrian Reith, managing director of Commercial Breaks, 'advertising is novelty, it's not boring or lulling the audience.' On a recent television chat show, a well-known actor of the 'London circuit' joked that he was much more embarrassed being caught doing voice-overs than being seen smoking, and that it was an absolute definition of money for old rope – turning up, saying 'soft, long and very, very strong', and then going out and buying a shirt with the money. While Steve Nallon finds that voice-overs can sometimes be a nightmare. He collects nonsensical sayings of producers, such as, 'Could you do it quicker but make it slower at the end?', 'Put a bit more red into it,' and 'A bit gritty, but be sympathetic'. He also warns that TV voice-overs can be 'an enclosed industry for a small number of actors'.

Which voices get the bookings? There is a flexible actor much in demand who is known in the industry as 'The Man Of Five Hundred Voices'. A famous voice can be connected to a brand, as Orson Welles with sherry. Steve Nallon comments somewhat iron-ically on voice-overs, particularly for TV, 'Most popular are rich, husky voices – the sort that seem to have smoked eighty cigarettes a day and drunk a lot. The sort who say, "you feed a voice". I'm more character than hard-sell.' The problem is as actor David Holt says, 'In many cases, voice-overs are absolutely instant. You don't see the scripts beforehand. There's a pile of them when you go into the studio and you work your way through.' The reason you don't see the script till you walk in is that everything is last-minute in the advertising industry. Adrian Reith explains. 'No normal person would believe the amount of last-minute changes. It's not so good for the actor starting out.' So you have to interpret a script instantly and change your approach within a minute.

For the 'London circuit', you dress casually, neither up nor down, maybe jeans and shirt. If you dress formally, you mark your-self out as a newcomer, and if you dress up too much, warns Ralph van Dijk, 'you'll look like you're earning more than us and we'll resent you! Be clean and don't smell!' The producer introduces you to the clients, who are usually middle to junior management. Mandy Wheeler recommends, 'Don't be frightened and don't sneer at them. If you do commercials, you have to get your attitude straightened out. But don't take rubbish from the clients and remember that they are the lay members, they are the audience to an extent. They may not have the vocabulary for their judgements and you usually hear, "I just didn't like that". So you respond, "I'll find a way to make it work for you." Be pro-active.' Adrian Reith knows of a good actor, 'but he gives off the wrong vibes to clients, he has a surly exterior, and his agent has told him to fix it.' Adrian also warns, 'Ad agencies have so many pressures that they like working with relaxed people. Sometimes enormous rows blow up in the session and the last thing they need is an angst-ridden actor in the corner.' Ralph van Dijk adds, 'Don't ask clients for freebies or discounts – it happens too often.'

The first thing you do with the script is to read it and mark it up. Think it through once and twice. Again, Mandy Wheeler: 'Ask your-self, what is the structure of the script? Beginning, middle and end, create it for yourself.' Dynamic or dreary as written copy, you have to ensure every word makes its impact in the least amount of time. Steve Nallon was once confronted with a carpets commercial. 'I had not the slightest idea of what the script said. The text was gram-matically impossible, and the task was to get all the words in the right order and hope for the best. It seemed to destroy any meaning, but I had to get the words over, and that's what they want.' For Mark Baggett, Head of Commercial Production, Dragon Radio, 'Not everything we do is art! There's a lot of "Great pine furniture sale is now on...".' Adrian Reith explains the impoverished script, 'It's been watered down by committee or it's half-baked because the clients don't go with it. Actors who are pros understand and I confide in them, and distance myself from what they have to do, because my job is to be a politician and get it through. A friend of mine calls directing commercials "turd-gilding".'

Character

The first type of script has you cast as a character, either single-voice or dialogue. Single-voice can be confiding, like the middle-aged woman saying, 'My friend Jack was looking for low-cost motor insurance, so he called...', or jokey, or blokey, or sincere. Whatever, there will always be a key emotion and you have to find the character's situation. Among countless examples of dialogue are the boss and office-boy, and teacher and class. For Mandy Wheeler, who directed actors before she started her company, 'My main note is play it for real, these are not cartoons. It's characterization, so you need motivation and even substitution if there's somebody the other side of the microphone, where you turn the other actor into someone you know. I make the actors do pre-scene work, just as for stage. It's even more important for commercials. It's as if the camera swings round and discovers you. Make the audience believe that there was something happening there before the script starts and there's something there afterwards. You have to create a character who is talking unreal stuff like, "Mmm! This is the greatest breakfast cereal I have ever had," and yet not allow the audience feel "Oh! It's an ad, I'm not interested in that". That's what I say in my classes to advertising creatives, using actors, because I believe that commercials are drama in one minute.' Mark Baggett also builds up scenes. 'For a comedy skit based on *The Bill*, I say, "You've jumped out of a car and you're banging on the flat door".' Adrian Reith finds 'audiences and actors relate to characters best and that's what we try to cast. We have an office joke about the "Voice of Death", the voice that ends up sounding like an announcer and not a proper actor, reading the copy as if he does not understand it.'

Single-voice announcement

The second category, the single-voice announcement script, or announcer, has copy like, 'Are you sure you are getting the best out of your life insurance?...' or 'Having a weekend in London? Then get around the easy way with the Weekend Travel Card...' Many writers and producers tend away from announcers because they find them faceless but the skill is to make the announcer a character too, in their own individual way, and 'to speak clearly and quickly, without sounding like that, with clear diction but making it sound natural,' as Ralph van Dijk summarizes. The announcer who has the 'chocolate' or 'deep-brown' voice is rather old-fashioned now, and notoriously difficult as it is to find a vocabulary for voice types, producers talk, for example, of light, mid-range, deep, sincere and youthful. Ralph also advises to emphasize the adjectives mostly, with the proviso that commercials are full of adjectives. The announcer also has to put over the product name convincingly and each time it occurs, without the ornament of dialogue or characterization. Ralph notes, 'The first time round, make room to introduce it and also the last time round. Be reassuring and confident, and make it seem a solid and believable product. Just give it that normal stress as if talking to the person next to you.' Adrian Reith finds, 'it'll stick out in the script, so make it conversational.' Mike Bersin, creative director of Emap Radio, believes, 'It's an old cliché but it's true – smile or wink when you say it and that will be heard in your voice.' Martyn Healey, Head of Commercial Production, Metro FM, gives the note, 'Imagine that everyone has heard of this product and loves it to death. Clear but not over the top.' Mandy Wheeler still uses the term actor for the single-voice announcement script because, 'all you have in commercials are characters, that's my belief.' Announcer roles often go, not to actors, but to others who work in radio as DJs and commercial producers themselves.

End-line

The final category, delivering the end-line, demands special technique and there are some actors who just cannot bring it off. An example of an end-line is, 'National Lottery Lucky Dip – it could be you. Players must be sixteen and over.' Adrian Reith puts it this way, 'The difficulty is that there is no known situation in life where someone comes out of the woodwork and says an end-line. It's the hardest thing on earth and we expend time and effort on it. There's a circuit of actors in London who can do it and they make a fortune.' Mandy Wheeler explains, 'You are there as the voice of the product. So I ask you what attitude do you have, why do you say this? Are you conspiratorial, friendly? Have a reason for saying this.' The end-line is also known as the strap-line or tag-line, both Americanisms.

The task of the actor in commercials is 'to fit that many words into that space in that order', as Adrian Reith says. 'My main note is: make me feel this – make me feel frightened or angry or friendly here.' All good producers encourage feedback from an actor and suggestions for minor changes are welcome, especially in what will read more smoothly. Ralph van Dijk adds, 'Treat the microphone as the person sitting opposite you. If you talk *at* them, they'll move away. Talk *to* them and they'll listen.'

Mandy Wheeler alerts actors new to the commercial studio, 'Some people directing may not know what they're doing and you have to do a lot of work yourself, more than on stage. Also, avoid what I call "inflection sickness", an up-and-down intonation, which some actors catch after doing commercials for a while.' She also adds realistically, 'Advertising people have the money to get it right. Either they'll work you flat out or they'll get someone else in and revoice it. It's about having technique and not just a nice voice. You also have to realize when you have become habituated to something, as after the seventh take. Stop, take a walk and get back to it freshly. And always ask for playback to hear yourself.' Peter Rinne, producer of his own company, Isis Duplicating, comments on 'the number of famous actors who have thrown their hands in the air for what they are being asked to do', and that with agency people and clients, 'everybody has to have their say, and you have fifty takes and the final one is take two'. Mark Baggett finds he works better in the studio with the actor, 'I keep good eye-contact and encourage with nods.'

Your show-reel

The last advice is about your show reel and Ralph van Dijk warns against being taken in by 'cheapo demo-tape specialists who give you an hour or more in the studio and five scripts, but who do not highlight your strengths.' All producers recommend careful research to choose scripts for appropriate products for which you hope to get casting. First on the tape should be your own speaking voice, simply saying who you are and your agent, and then demonstrate your main strength. What you demonstrate should be consistent, and each commercial should be thirty seconds. Martyn Healey instructs, 'Don't use made-up clients and scripts. We want to know that you've done it before for real. Some of the best show reels manage to tell a story with one actor doing all the parts. The opening needs to be strong without being sycophantic or patronising.'

Ralph van Dijk warns against doing impressions, or only one or two at most, because they have a limited use. 'If a living person is impersonated in a commercial without their permission, they'll sue the pants off the company.' Tapes sent in unsolicited go to the bottom of the pile in many offices; whereas, it is assumed that having an agent means an actor has been vetted already and been taken seriously. Ralph adds, 'And if you have sent in a tape, don't call! And certainly not again and again! I will be turned off using you.' Adrian Reith finds that a major mistake in show reels is that the actor displays 'every accent under the sun and we're bored with that. I don't want to hear your Yorkshire followed by your Cornish. The people who can do that are very rare and they blow you away, like John Sessions. Advertising people are very cynical and not easily entertained, so don't make it jokey.' You have to do your own research for your show reel by: listening to radio and TV, deciding what of your strengths to display; and by showing yourself as character, announcer and delivering the end-line. Mike Bersin, creative director of Emap Radio, gives an example of the worst show reel posted in. 'A terribly correct 1950s voice intoned, "I will now read selections from *The Punic Wars*", and then did so, at length! My advice is to follow up your show reel with phone calls but find a palatable way of presenting yourself to your potential customers.' Martyn Healey remembers, 'We were once impressed enough by a show tape to give the guy some work only to discover when in the studio that he had a lisp. His demo tape managed to avoid the use of words containing the letter "s"!'

The revolution in the commercial market to actors' home studios has 'made it even more difficult for actors to get into the business', says Mark Baggett. 'It's better if you explain with your voice tape that you will be prepared to drive to the station in ten minutes or for such and such amount of money. But producers tend to pick up the phone and if I have nine actors I can contact, the first one who says, "I can do it now," will get the job. The good news is that the radio market is expanding and could well grow by 25% each year. I need young voices with skills, as for club ads, voices that sound street-cred, happening. Are they teaching these skills to training actors? If not, why not?'

It is useful to note some of the points that are used to sell radio advertising to its potential customers and I rely here, gratefully, on booklets distributed by The Radio Advertising Bureau (RAB). Radio is close to the consumer and is informal, and so is able to 'secure a more central place for the brand in consumers' lives'. By contrast with TV, radio commercials are less obviously flagged and set apart, which means the listener will not screen them out so easily or switch over. People *hear* the TV, but *listen* to the radio with more attention, especially before they go out to work and to shop. Voice and music convey more emotion and mood, and trigger memories. In an article for the RAB giving examples of good and bad commercials, Simon Waldman selected as his pits and hits: the Iberian Airlines' 'Try us, fly us', spoken in a solemn business voice, as a lame end-line, and by contrast, an Imperial War Museum commercial, simply featuring a letter sent by a soldier to his parents the day before he died, as brilliantly effective.

Check list: commercial voice-over

Play it for real and avoid the old-fashioned 'hard sell' and 'soft sell'.

Always ask for playback and get it precisely right – your commercial is going to be heard more than once!

Respect the commercial studio teamwork.

BOOK READINGS, AUDIO BOOKS AND STORY READINGS

You work about six or seven hours per day, sitting in a small studio.

Production is either 'rock-and-roll', a self-editing faster system, or record and edit in post-production.

Angela Pleasence sums up technique for book and story readings. 'You have to arrive absolutely with it ready and the director has to do little directing. I colour code the characters – in one book about vicars and tea parties, I counted forty-three different voices, mostly men, from silly teenagers to the very old.' Remember that in addition to all the speaking characters for whom you have to discover distinct voices, you have to create the character of the narrator and this may take some exploration with the producer (less often called the director here).

Preparation is essential for the team. Jane Morgan says: 'You have to write down a list of the characters and avoid the embarrassment of getting to page one hundred and fifty in the studio and finding that some man has a slight Swedish accent! As producer you have to know the details for your actors and is Uncle Charlie the fat one or the thin one?' Working on an unabridged book, which could amount to twelve cassettes of ninety minutes each, actress Jacqueline King does her homework during the three weeks before the studio when she receives the script. 'I look for references to how the characters speak, sparkily or gruffly or such, and find all the dialects, Irish, American, Canadian. I even had to voice a Swahili warrior.'

Studio production schedules depend on different methods and budgets. For unabridged books, the working day is nine to five, with an hour for lunch, taking an average of four days. For all audio books, production is designed around each side of the cassette, and the producer may have the actor slow down or speed up to fit in with this because each of the completed sides must match up in length, even though the actor may feel it goes against the text. Everyone finds the intense concentration required a burden, creative though the work is. As Peter Rinne puts it, 'My job as producer is to fit everything together like a jigsaw, and create a working environment for actor and publisher. The actor has the hard end of the job. There are wonderful readers in this country, the talent is mind-boggling.'

Self-editing

Rock-and-roll is much the cheaper and faster working system and demands a lot more of the actor in speed. It is a self-editing system as you go along and post-production time is enormously reduced. When there is a fluff or the producer interrupts with a note on the talkback, the tape is wound back to the beginning of the paragraph and the actor has to resume or 'drop in' as it is called. To drop in, the actor listens to the previous short section, on cans or on the studio speaker, and pays careful attention to tempo, pitch patterning and breathing, so all matches up. It is sometimes useful to mouth along and then carry on at the cue. Other problems that can hold up a production are tummy rumbling, mouth clicks and odd breathing. Post-production now becomes a cleaning-up operation and with a very fluent actor, there can be three hours product from four hours in the studio. Jane Morgan says, 'I don't find it the ideal system, though the last two audio books I directed, with Frances Tomelty and Molly Keane, were the ones I admire most.'

Record and edit in post-production

The second method is record and edit in post-production, and the old rule was that one hour in the studio involved two hours in post-production. Obviously, the actor still has to have the ability to drop in and to resume with the flow after a break. No producer likes to 'hit the button', to interrupt with a note and impose his or her idea on the performance. It may become necessary for all the obvious reasons, but especially if the meaning does not come through or if an emphasis is missed. Peter Rinne gives the cautionary tale of Ian McKellen in the studio, 'At a point he gave an unusual reading, not what I would have imagined and it would have been wrong for me to stifle it. But the editor instructed me to stop him, so I said over the talkback, "We have a little query here," and received a flat "No" in reply. You could feel a distinct chilling in the studio.'

Jane Morgan finds the notes she gives most often are, 'Too large for a reading' and 'You've lost the character there'. Radio 4 book episodes have more time in the studio, usually one hour for fifteen minutes of broadcast time; or for a ten-part *Book at Bedtime,* for example, three days in production. Director Pam Brighton in Belfast does all the talking she needs to do at the beginning and says, 'I go for experienced and intelligent actors anyway, those I can be confident in. Edna O'Brien the novelist completed all ten parts in the one day because she has a huge energy and she knew her own book intimately.' If the first episode is not good enough, often a director will go back at the end and rerecord, and some BBC directors will record the rehearsals as well. Peter Rinne finds the greatest difficulty can be with an actor who is too self-critical. 'You can get through a twenty-minute section with no problem and after one mistake, the actor gets worked up and destroys his own environment.' While Tessa Worsley admits, 'It's very hard to read a book you don't like, so much harder than on stage where at least you are supported; and what is the technique? Sheer determination.'

Actors find that with rock-and-roll and commercial pressures, producers look out for technical aspects, such as accuracy, popping and sibilants, and infrequently give artistic notes. With audio books, the completed recording is sent for proof-reading to outside listeners, who are experts in the field, as in dialect etc. The actor returns to the studio to make corrections by lifting out a paragraph and newly voice-matching it, taking care to create the same studio conditions. Jilly Bond finds that a mistake crops up about once a book and sometimes not at all. Some publishers pay a flat fee per audio book, for example £650 in total for a twelve-cassette book, taking four days in the studio; while others pay a fee, of say £700, plus royalties.

Getting started in radio drama

To get acting work on radio, you nearly always have to be a member of Equity. Although technically the closed shop has gone, BBC Radio will not employ anyone without an Equity card. Caroline Raphael, Head of Radio Drama, said, 'Not my decision, by the way!' In exceptional circumstances, the director or producer can employ others if a good case can be put to the Equity Conciliation meeting. Apply for auditions by sending in your voice tape with a letter and a photo. Workshops for eight actors at a time are organized in London about every three months and each region holds its own auditions. Some actors are asked to join the Radio Drama Company directly from these. In workshops, actors demonstrate their range across four or five short pieces and sight-reading.

Research: Start recording plays from the radio. Replay and listen professionally to the more interesting ones. Discover the whole range of BBC radio plays across the four channels. See where you think you fit in. Buy the *Radio Times* every week and note the credits for actors and directors (or producers), and what particular work they do. Keep back copies and research more about the radio business. Find out if your local radio stations ever broadcast plays, even if only rarely. This is all part of your career 'networking' as an actor. Listen to all radio performers, from DJs to chat shows to news readers; consider their technique and what makes them good or not so good.

No-fee, low-fee work: Get into the audio books market by no-fee or low-fee work for charity organizations such as the Royal National Institution for the Blind.

Attend BBC Radio light entertainments and panel recordings: You get tickets from the BBC Ticket Unit. They advertise regularly or you can phone and inquire. Sit at the front and watch technique.

With more independent productions under the 10% quota, find out about recording elsewhere, sometimes in stand-up comedy venues.

Student productions: Try to get into student radio productions in college and university media/drama courses. Phone around for courses to contact. These take place September to June, with more advanced work usually in the period March to June. Take your own initiative here as courses rarely import actors in the way television and film courses do and they do not have similar production budgets. But the way into film is through student films and corporate videos, so you should try gaining studio experience and extending your *c.v.* and portfolio in student radio. Try to network with working radio actors in the way you should with actors in the other media. Many radio performers, presenters and DJs, have started in hospital radio.

Be selective: Do not send every director a voice tape. Select a director for his or her work and let them know what you have to offer. Include a photo.

Pam Brighton, director BBC Northern Ireland:
I'm always taken by how surprised first-time actors are. The only crime in the studio is rustling the script. I typecast for radio. Actors have to have credibility on radio, like film, so I cast people close to who they are. I rarely have time to listen to voice tapes. It is kind of worthwhile sending them in to me because I file them under different voices, such as 'Kerry' etc. Do your voice tape only in your own accent. I hear tapes which run the gamut of every accent known to man. My advice is to reflect you and your strengths, I'm not looking for technical proficiency in dialects.

David Hitchinson, director World Service, Bush House, London:
It's the same as theatre, you have to knock on doors. It helps if people write to me and keep me informed, but don't get in touch if you have got nothing to say. It helps to listen to plays and to know what you are talking about. There is little I can tell from a voice tape and I know that sounds brutal, though I or my excellent PA listen to them all. A big industry is building up around voice tapes.

Jeremy Mortimer, director, Broadcasting House:
Get an idea of which producers do the best work and write to ask 'could I see you?' A voice tape has to be very short and well done – not rambling and badly recorded. We need people who have worked

for two years professionally and who fit with our current criteria. We have run workshops recently for disabled actors and black actors.

Stuart Richards, producer for independent Mr Punch Productions:
We try to discourage actors sending in voice tapes and we need to create our own repertory company in the future. The best place for a young actor to carve a niche is voice-over work or in the RDC. Independent companies always employ ex-BBC directors who are liable to cast actors who have worked at the BBC.

Jilly Bond, previously in the RDC:
In my first job I had to have an orgasm for forty-five seconds. I remember watching the clock and it got quite difficult at the end.

Moir Leslie actress:
I find radio drama is not rated by certain casting directors. When I contact them about broadcasts, they say, 'What can we possibly tell from listening?' Another national company casting director said, 'I'm always using radio actors in little bits and pieces.'

Jonathan Taffler, actor:
I had no training, but no formal training as an actor either. My first impression of the radio studio, in 1986, was a sense of panic at the speed. You have to get on top quickly and it could be a new play or a dense classic. I was amazed at how good the other actors were and how very quick they were at 'committing'. On stage, you nerve yourself up to have a go through three weeks rehearsal.

David Holt, actor previously in RDC:
I started in 1981 in hospital radio, with voice-over work, commercials and producing, for Liverpool's Radio City, IR. At the Birmingham School of Speech and Drama, in the three-year course, I learned basic microphone technique and I came down to BH to record as a winner in the Carlton Hobbs Award. Then I was in Coventry's CWR (BBC local radio) experimental soap, *Hillcrest*, which had a Health Authority link-in. I got Pebble Mill contracts, averaging one play a month and then the RDC.

James Aubrey, actor:
It always surprises me how well-known actors get into the studio for the first time and they kick off like a 21-year-old. It's marvellous. I've just been working with Joanna Lumley in her first radio play.

Kerry Shale, actor:

I started in a large-cast play in Bristol for four days, in 1980, under Brian Miller, the sort of scale they can't do now, thrown in at the deep end, with a range of small parts. I learnt by my first radio kiss, with a young actress after lunch on the first day. It was a romantic twosome, on a buggy and buckboard, and we did jostling buckboard acting, gently up and down. I thought a radio kiss meant you kiss your wrist and make wet noises. Brian Miller came on the talkback, and said, 'You know how we do it in this country? For real!' So this actress who I hardly knew and I did the kiss for 'real', scraping our teeth together. The actors told me later, 'Brian was having you on.' We were totally innocent. It's taken years to gain radio skills. Overplaying was never a problem for me. I used to be of the 'Peter Barkworth school of acting' and I followed his book, but now, I don't at all. My script used to be full of squiggles and markings, pauses indicated, etc. Stress the second syllable and all. So when I got to my first lead part, it was awash with instructions. I worked it out beforehand and if I recreated it, I was satisfied. Over the years since, I've gradually rejected all that. I walk in with a blank script and take the director's notes, and give myself some more. I write in pauses, I work on instinct, not technique. I've got the technique, God knows, so what else is there? I'm doing the same in my stage and TV work now. Technique holds you back. So I read the script a couple of times and I wing it. I find there's plenty of time in the radio studio for that.

Finale

The radio audience is the actor too

It has been said that performing without a public is like playing tennis without a net. A live theatre audience gives continuous feedback. It is not just their laughter and excitement, and their shuffling and coughing when bored, but there is a continuous extra-sensitive dialogue going back-and-forth across the footlights. Stage actors can even sense the audience's collective breathing and so gain a moment-to-moment verdict. The theatre audience is a group while the radio listeners are addressed as individuals. I have discussed earlier how isolated radio actors seem to be in the studio and how cut off from their future audience. But everything they do is for the radio audience 'out there'. Those listeners are the final arbiters of the play, and though there is not enough feedback from them, some of their applause and – more likely – their brickbat letters, trickle through to the radio management.

Every production choice is for the listeners, about the listeners and how they listen. Radio listeners are obviously a different category of audience to theatre-goers and viewers of films and TV, as in receiving the play aurally they become more actively engaged. They have to manufacture their own visual images in response to what they hear, and to run, in their minds, their own radio 'cinema' for the succession of broadcast sound pictures. Some listeners visualize character's faces in detail and can 'see' the dialogue. Every listener gets a different play and one that they have 'co-authored' in a way. That is partly why they are so loyal and feel the plays are so much part of their living environment. The fact is that the radio audience do more of their own work and 'own' more of the play.

Stage actors refer to their audience as being the 'final actor', an obvious truth. The play ends up with them and they are the final critics. As an actor, you have to surrender the sum of the meaning and the product to them, and to let go. What does this mean for you as a radio actor? At times it means accepting that 'less is more' (see Chapter 7). Character and social stereotypes, or categories to use a more neutral term, can come over more satisfyingly on radio. No more sketching in is needed for a cameo part and the listener can quickly supply the face, hair, clothes, shoes and lifestyle on your first 'entrance'. Immediately they can flesh out how that character – traveller, student, pensioner, jogger, gardening neighbour, adulterer – looks. You do not always need to spotlight a particular trait in dialect or attitude.

It can perhaps mean that you have to go for the obvious choices, even though your training and stage experience have told you to act 'against the part'. That is, to search for a minor characteristic and bring that to the fore to make the character more complex and less stereotyped. What you have on your side is the listener's powerful sense of hearing. We have five senses (at least), and hearing is the first that is developed in the womb where the baby lives in a sound world. The mother's heartbeat has a frequency of 70 and the foetus's is about 140. Being born means being thrust into sound chaos of the outside. Hearing is part of our primitive vigilance system, to alert us to danger.

You can exercise the most extraordinary story-telling power over your listeners. You can whisper to them, soothe them, frighten them and enter into the secret part of their minds. The rhythm of your dialogue can be as effective as music, and be combined with the music beats, and you catch listeners at that biological first base. You can bring friendship and dialogue into their lives and you may be the only humane and friendly talk they have all day. Being a radio listener is an experience that is both remote, because radio is blind and broadcast to us from afar, and intimate, because voices create the dialogue, seemingly 'interactive' experience. Listen to how Terry Wogan creates apparently two-way dialogue every morning on Radio 2.

We know that the best theatre is where there is less distance between performer and spectator, and where the nuances of face and body can be clearly experienced. A theatre seating 500 is the best for the sort of 'talkie' plays long the tradition in Europe. Ibsen and Ayckbourn come over best if you are in the front stall seats and not up in the gods, or, as Dame Edna Everidge calls it, the 'ash-tray'. Since our main theatres are larger than this, a lot of the audience get less of the play. Radio listeners always get the best seats for your performance and indeed, can be placed in the middle of the action where even your character's breathing is felt. And as in real life, when another person comes too close in speaking to us and we fear they are trying to control us, or we welcome them into our space, what is called our 'body bubble', so your radio character can 'invade' the listener powerfully. While even the best theatre seat is physically fixed in one place with a single view of the total stage space, your listener changes his or her perspective constantly. Radio can 'zoom in' and enter the mind of the character, and then give the whole sound picture of everybody in the scene.

So, as a radio character, you can become closer than the film close-up. It is your voice directly into your listeners' minds. You allow them to 'play' with you. Let the audience be the 'final actor' who finishes off every scene.

Appendix I: Technical Terms

Accent (voice): (1) dialect; (2) emphasis

Acoustics: (1) study of the behaviour of sound; (2) in an enclosed space such as a recording studio, the combination of direct and indirect sounds reaching the microphone, along with modifications such as screens and curtains

Across the Microphone: *see* oblique microphone

Actuality: (1) recording the actual sound of an event as opposed to the artificial conditions of a studio; (2) (television) recording news events

Ambience: (1) natural background noise in every environment from a busy street to a quiet studio; (2) background noise indicating location in a radio play scene, the equivalent of background track in film

Analogue Recording: recording on magnetic tape

Anechoic: *see* dead studio

Announcer (commercial): type of radio commercial where the actor works with a single-voice announcement script

'Archers' Fade: traditional fade to black and fade in again, so called from its use in *The Archers*

Articulation (voice): clarity and accuracy in the voice stream

At-a-run: less usual production system in radio drama, where the play is rehearsed and then recorded as a whole, as opposed to rehearse-record

Attack: onset of a sound event, followed by its decay

Atmos or Atmosphere: (1) (radio drama) the sound of voices in a particular location; (2) (radio drama) pre-recorded atmos as of street traffic; (3) background sound in any location

AudioFile: computerised sound editing system used in radio, as also Sadie

Balance: (1) placing of microphones and sound sources, such as actors, relative to each other in the studio; (2) mixing of sound events and their levels against each other by the Studio Manager; (3) distribution of sound in stereo between left and right (and middle)

Basic Production: (coined by author) production not in the larger and more expensive studio suite and either with more modest resources or with smaller, professional portable equipment

Bass Tip-up: exaggeration of bass in voice caused by the speaker, usually male, being close to the microphone

Biography (actor): character's life details, including 'pre-text', before the play events begin

Bit the Cue (actor): taking up your cue smartly (an American term)

Black: silence between scenes, usually of two to three seconds, as in 'fade to black'

Blasting: distortion caused by too loud a volume of voice

Blocking: physical movements and positions for the actor around the microphone

Boxy: sounding as in an enclosed and small acoustic, for example, a prison cell

Brand Name (commercial): the product name in a commercial

Bright: sounding as in a reflective acoustic, also live

Brown voice: old-fashioned male voice with a warm, resonantal bass, especially in commercials

Cans: headphones

Cardioid (microphone): type of microphone with the field in a broad heart shape. See Appendix III, page 163.

Centre: (1) (voice) middle of the voice's pitch range also termed habitual pitch; (2) (actor) psychological and balancing mid-point of the body into which energy flows and out of which energy is directed

Character (commercial): type of work in commercials where the actor is cast as a character, in dialogue or single-voice

Cheat: to fake some action in performance, as slowing it down or speeding it up, or cutting out some small portions of it; for example on stage, eating and drinking

Clustering (voice): (coined by author) in a radio drama scene, too great a similarity between voices where the listener cannot readily identify one character from another

Cocktail-party Effect: ability of the brain-ear mechanism to pick out a speaker from the hubbub all around, so called from the situation of holding a conversation in a cocktail party

Colour (voice): added personality and detail given to a character's voice by the radio actor, as for example, by embodying

Control Cubicle: (old BBC radio term) production room for the director, Studio Manager and other technicians where studio and prerecorded sound is mixed, balanced and recorded

Control Panel: sound mixing desk in the charge of the Studio Manager (panel SM)

Copy (commercial): script in commercials

Crash In On (actor): coming in on a scene partner's line before they finish speaking and so masking some of their words

Close-up or CU (film): camera term for tight shot – shoulders and face

Cue Light: red light for recording and green for 'go'

Cut: (1) the order to stop action; (2) anything cut from the script

Dead Air: unexplained silence in broadcast

Dead Studio: special radio drama studio, also called anechoic, in which sound is damped down by absorbant or padded surfaces on walls and ceiling, and often used for 'outside' scenes

Dead: area of studio where sound is absorbed to a greater extent

Description: (coined by author) scripted extra in radio drama to compensate for the blind medium, putting across physical details, expressions and movements, etc.

Dialect (voice): aspects of a speaker's voice which indicate geographical region, sex, social class, age and subgroup to which he or she belongs

Diaphragm (microphone): crucial working part of a microphone, a surface which is mechanically shifted in response to sound waves

Digital (recording): system of sound recording where the sound is encoded into digital or number sequences, as opposed to the older analogue system, and allowing more accuracy and treatment by computerised systems

Drop In (book readings): *see* rock-and-roll

Embodying (actor): (coined by author) representing physical movement and presence in radio acting

End-line (commercial): the final selling line in the commercial script

Endowing (actor): an actor's technique which consists of imaginatively adding to the scene partner some feature or other from the character they are playing to gain the 'reality' of the scene, and so a lesser form of substitution

Establishing Shot (film): a wide camera shot that shows the viewers the location of the scene

Extreme Close-up or ECU (film): very tight shot as on a actor's mouth

Fader: a slider on the control panel or sound mixing desk, which raises the volume on a channel or takes it out again; and also called a potentiometer or pot

Fade in: bring up the volume of sound from zero level

Fade out: take out the volume of sound

Fade To Black: take out the volume of sound to silence

Field (microphone): microphone's working area

Figure-of-eight (microphone): type of microphone with the field in a figure-of-eight shape. See Appendix III, page 163.

Filmic directing style: (coined by author) type of directing and production in radio drama which uses filming techniques, either in director's notes to the actors or in creative style

Final Actor (as in 'the audience is the final actor'): a saying by actors, meaning that the audience is the final arbiter of the play

First Audience (film): while filming, those alongside the camera witnessing the actor's performance and who can give some feedback and support

Five Positions at the Microphone: (coined by author) first position – as near the microphone as possible for interiorising or 'thoughts'; second position – a few inches away, for intimate dialogue; third position – an arm's length away, for normal conversation; fourth position – a couple of steps or more further off and halfway to the 'door', in the imaginary 'room'; fifth position – moves off

Flickered out: quick flicks on the cue light to signal to the actors that the sequence is over

Fluff: verbal slip

Foldback: sound effects or music fed into the studio by speakers and so recorded within the sound set and its acoustic, an example being pop music in a teenager's bedroom or a tannoy announcement

FXs: pre-recorded sound effects

Given Circumstances: (originating from Stanislavski) the details of the dramatic situation

Glottal Stop (voice): removing the final 't' of a word before another word beginning with a vowel, or before all vowels, as in Cockney dialect – 'a be- [glottal stop] -er bi- [glottal stop] of bu- [glottal stop] -er' for 'a better bit of butter'

'Going for levels' or 'Let's take some for levels': the actor is requested to voice some script allowing the Studio Manager to adjust the sound levels for recording

Grams SM: (old BBC term) sound technician who cues in pre-recorded effects, usually on CDs

Green Light: for 'go', i.e. start recording

Green Room: retiring room for actors

Habitual Pitch (voice): *see* centre

Head Focus or Head Concentration: (coined by author) correct positioning of the head in relation to the microphone

Head Moves: (coined by author) movements of the head in relation to the microphone and in the switch from one microphone position to another

Hook: first thirty seconds of a radio play which must engage the listener's attention

Hypercardioid (microphone): type of microphone with the field in a broader heart shape than the cardiod. See Appendix III, page 163.

Hyperventilating (voice): unwelcome panting and over-exciting of the breathing mechanism due to exertion by the actor, and so interfering with performance

Improvisation or Improv: actors create dialogue and actions from a suggested situation

In the Can: the recording of a section of script is completed

Inbreath (voice): drawing in the breath

Inside-out: (originating with Stanislavski, as in 'working inside-out') creating characterisation by first working from the mind of the character; also called the cerebral or psychological approach. *See* outside-in.

Interiorizing or 'thoughts': (coined by author) the character's inner voice or ruminations, often performed in position one at the microphone, and these can be short or extend to a whole monologue

Into the Dead (microphone – mono): stepping out of the microphone's field in mono

Intonation (voice): *see* pitch

Intonation Contour (voice): pitch variations in talk which make patterns with rising and falling, like the contours of a map showing hills and valleys

Intonation Pattern (voice): *see* Intonation Contour

ISDN (Integrated Services Digital Network) (phone line): a specially installed phone line which transmits a higher quality signal of professional quality for broadcast and used by actors with home studios for commercials

Keeping In (actor): ability to maintain presence in the scene while others are speaking

Key Word (actor): a technique of preparation using key words or phrases from the script and repeating them before the cue light comes on

Larynx (voice): voice box at the top of the windpipe

Lavalier (microphone): small personal microphone worn round the neck or attached to a lapel

Live Studio: where most recording takes place and called 'live' because the sound reverberates off various surfaces

London Circuit (commercial): top end of commercials production, mostly in central London studios

Long Shot or LS (film): the actor's whole body is in frame

Mark: (1) (film) the mark on the studio floor indicating where the actor stands; (2) (radio) where the actor should stand

Marking Up Script (actor): actor's notes written on the script which include comments by director. See Appendix II, page 162.

Mask (sound): sound events which cover over or obliterate others as in the visual masking on stage of one actor by another

Medium Close-up or MCU (film): a shot that is not as tight as a close-up

Medium Shot or MS (film): closer than a long shot

Mixing: combining of output from various sound channels on the control panel (sound mixing desk)

Moment (actor): portions of the script which, though small in extent, demand especial detail in the acting, as reflected in the actors' advice 'don't lose out on the moment'

Mono or Monophonic Sound: sound heard from one channel and two-dimensional in its representation of space and movement, forward and backward, and without a sideways spread, as opposed to stereo

Moves (actor): (1) moving around, and away from and approaching the microphone; (2) 'moves off' is position 5

Narrator's Mike: a sound set where you are close-miked and surrounded by screens

Neutral Acoustic: little distinctive is heard of a location's acoustic around the voice of the actor and used, for example, with narrator's mike

OB or Outside Broadcast: recording outside the studio

Object of Attention (actor): (originating with Stanislavski) a real or imaginary object on which the actor's attention is focused in performance on stage

Oblique Microphone: in microphone position no 1, where the actor is placed sideways on to the microphone, to avoid blasting and popping

Opened-out (radio director's style): (coined by author) a wider sound set, affording the actors greater freedom to move around, as opposed to the up-front style

Optimum Pitch (voice): the most efficient range of pitch notes in the voice

Out of Phase (microphone – stereo): stepping out of the microphone's field

Outbreath (voice): letting out the breath

Outside-In (actor): (originating with Stanislavski) creating characterisation by first working from the character's outside or body, movements and walk; also called the somatic approach. *See* inside-out.

PA: production assistant who works with the director, contacting actors in pre-production and note-taking in production

Panel SM: *see* studio manager

Paralanguage (voice): literally in talk, the 'language around language', and so all the sighing, laughing, breathing, cries, 'aahs', etc. *See* umms.

Peak Emotions (actor): high level emotions

Perspective: (1) (painting and film) the depth in the visual field; (2) in sound and radio drama, the depth in the sound picture, and often organised as figure-and-ground – characters' voices against the background atmos

Physical Action (actor): a trigger in preparation by using a movement of the character coming into the scene or sequence, sometimes in an approach to the microphone

Pitch (voice): the singing aspect or the melody of the voice, also called range or intonation

Pitch Patterning (voice): *see* intonation contour

Pitching Up (voice): the unfortunate tendency of some actors to copy fellow actors' pitch

Playback: the playing back of a recorded sequence

Popping: microphone distortion caused by the plosive consonants B, P, D, T, G, K

Positions: *see* five positions at the microphone

Post-production: editing and everything else that is done when production is over

Pot (potentiometer): *see* fader

Pre-production: scripting, casting and all else that is done before production starts

Preparation (actor): techniques to prepare an actor before both a performance and a scene

Production: recording time in the studio

Programme: output from the control cubicle which is relayed into the studio by speakers and which cuts out before recording

Psychological Gesture (actor): a trigger in preparation by using a distinctive gesture of the character

Range (voice): *see* pitch

Rate (voice): *see* tempo

RDC: the BBC's repertory Radio Drama Company, traditionally called the 'Rep'

Reaction Shot (film): shot taken of an actor responding to another's lines

Reactions (voice): *see* umms

Read-Through: a reading through of the script by all the actors before production starts

Record and Edit (book readings): more expensive and traditional production system in book readings where more is left to post-production, as opposed to rock-and-roll

Red Light: recording in progress

Reflective Surface: sound surface which returns sound echoes or sound waves and also called bright

Rehearse-Record: most usual production method in radio drama, where production progresses from one sound set to another, sometimes out of sequence with the storyline, and opposed to at-a-run

Rep: *see* RDC

Research (commercial): radio commercial recorded for clients to decide on and not for broadcast

Resonance (voice): resonating tones caused by the resonator cavities, especially in the head and throat

Rhotacization (voice): imperfect 'r' sounded as a 'w'

Rock-and-Roll (book readings): faster self-editing production system in book readings where the tape is wound back to the beginning of the paragraph after a fluff, and the actor resumes or 'drops in', and so less is left to post-production

Rustling: making the radio script rustle or flap

Self-editing (book readings): faster self-editing system in production of book readings. *See* Rock-and-roll.

Sensory Imagination (actor): preparation technique to realise the scene's location and 'reality' through the five senses

Sequence: portion of script for a take, requiring its own set and smaller than a scene, usually

Set: set constructed in the studio with screens, curtains, floor coverings and microphones

Shift (actor): (coined by author) the move from one microphone position to another, requiring care, especially in head focus; also switch

Show Reel (commercial): audition tape containing five or so commercials

Sibilance (voice): overuse of 's'

Sound Centre: the central point around which the perspective of the sound picture is organised, either fixed or moving (*see* we go with)

Sound Picture: in the blind medium of radio drama, the aurally represented scene

Spot SM: technician who works in the studio creating Spot effects as with the Spot door, cups and steps

Standard Production: (coined by author) the most customary realist production style in BBC radio drama

Staying In: *see* keeping in

Stereo: three-dimensional sound picture

Stereo Pair: (1) two microphones set up in a 'V' pattern or across each other for stereo recording; (2) a stereo microphone which combines two in one. See Appendix III, page 163.

Studio Manager or Panel SM: chief sound technician in charge of the control panel

Studio Suite: combination of control cubicle, studio (live and sometimes also dead), and sometimes also a green room

Substitution (actor): (originating with Stanislavski) substituting for your co-partner in a scene an image of another person who more nearly resembles the character for you

Subtext (actor): the 'space between the words' of a script, the added details that an actor must bring to what is notated in the script, rounding out the character's psychology

Switch: *see* shift

Talkback: instructions relayed into the studio on speakers by the director or Studio Manager

Talking Heads: a phrase used in condemnation of a radio drama scene, as in 'that sounds too talking heads', and meaning that it is too static a stretch of dialogue, and that it does not represent sufficient movement and convincing physicality

Tempo (voice): speed of voice production, also rate. *See* word-strike

Thoughts: see interiorizing

Travel on the Line (actor): a director's instruction to continue speaking while moving or shifting from one microphone position to another

Turn (actor): swivelling body and head around from the waist and away from the microphone at moments of higher volume and so to avoid blasting

Umms (actor): reactions by the actor voiced while scene partners are speaking and usually in paralanguage, as 'aha'

Up-front (radio director's style): (coined by author) a more compact sound set, giving the actors tighter moves, as opposed to opened-up style

Visualisation (actor): the actor's ability to visualise mentally the details of the sound picture, to 'make it real', usually by sensory techniques

Voice-over: (1) (film) actor's voice that is heard over the picture; (2) (radio) actor's voice recorded for commercial; (3) narrator in film or TV

Voice Qualities (voice): distinctive elements which individualise a speaker's voice such as huskiness and which are also the result of the resonator mechanism

Voice Stream (voice): the continuous output of the voice

Voice Tape (commercials): *see* show reel

Volume (voice): amplitude of voice

We Go With (radio script): direction in a radio script that the action is continuous and moves, for example, with the imagined steps of the character 'up the garden path', a moving sound centre

Word Strike (voice): measure of pace of delivery by the number of words per minute (wpm)

Wrap: (film) shooting for the day is finished

Appendix II: Marking Up Your Script

There are some good hints in Peter Barkworth's *About Acting* for marking up your script and you can adapt your own system from the following. It is best to make use of brackets and underlining, so you do not confuse your notes with the script and written alterations to the script.

Moving around

(ɪ)   turn from the waist

①-⑤   microphone positions numbering one to five

Pitch

＼ falling pitch

／ rising pitch

V fall-rise

– level

~ rise-fall-rise

Pause, pace, emphasis

····   long pause

···   medium pause

I can't >do it now<	pace is quicker between the 'less than' signs
<u>*Hand*</u> *it over*	underlining gives emphasis
H̄ave it your own way	line over words means 'throw them away'
f	loudly
ff	very loudly
p	quietly
pp	very quietly or whisper
What ha:ppened to you	colon means prolong syllable preceding it
I'm so:: sorry	double colon means prolong even more
! and !! and even !!!	excitement

Breathing and laughing

(ʜ)   'H' as in 'huh' means an inbreath

(ʜₓ)   outbreath

☺   smile

☺   laugh

Miscellaneous

It's over to you and <u>your wife.</u>   crash into the end of your partner's line

It's over. I can't go on.   join up these sentences
    ᵛ

<u>(cough)</u> <u>(sniff)</u> <u>(snort)</u> <u>(falsetto)</u> <u>(whisper)</u> <u>(rustle clothes)</u> specifies actions

Appendix III: Microphones

A microphone is designed to have a directional response pattern and these diagrams show the field for each.

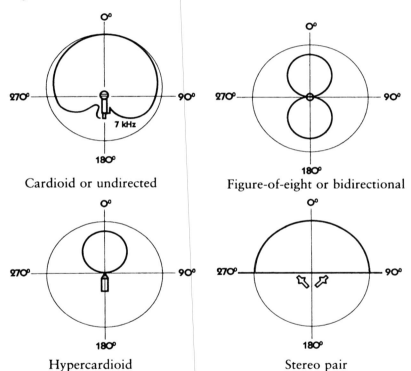

Cardioid or undirected

Figure-of-eight or bidirectional

Hypercardioid

Stereo pair

Appendix IV: Book List

Unfortunately, not many radio play scripts have been printed, particularly not those which reflect the regular output. A list is given in Rosemary Horstmann, *Writing for Radio* (A & C Black 1997).

Stephen Aaron, *Stage Fright, Its Role in Acting* (University of Chicago Press 1988)
William Ash, *The Way to Write Radio Drama* (Elm Tree Books 1985)
Peter Barkworth, *About Acting* (Secker & Warburg 1980)
Brian Bates, The Actor's Way (Boston 1987)
Robert Benedetti, *The Actor at Work* (Prentice-Hall 1970)
Michael Caine, *Acting in Film* (Applause Books 1997)
Andrew Crisell, *Understanding Radio* (Methuen 1986)
John Drakakis (ed.), *British Radio Drama* (CUP 1981)
Peter Lewis (ed.), *Radio Drama* (Longman 1981)
Jacqueline Martin, *Voice in Modern Theatre* (Routledge 1991)
Hugh Morrison, *Acting Skills* (A & C Black 1995)
Malcolm Morrison, *Clear Speech* (A & C Black 1977)
Patsy Rodenburg, *The Right to Speak* (Methuen 1992)
Ian Rodger, *Radio Drama* (Macmillan 1982)
J. Clifford Turner, revised by Malcolm Morrison, *Voice and Speech in the Theatre* (A & C Black 1995)

Appendix V: Useful Addresses

A full list of radio stations, both BBC and independent radio (IR), can be found in *Writers' & Artists' Yearbook* (A & C Black).

British Broadcasting Corporation (BBC)

BBC Corporate Headquarters and BBC Radio Broadcasting House, London WIA IAA Tel: 0171–580 4468
RADIO 1, Egton House, London, W1A 1AA Tel: 0171–765 4561
RADIO 2, BBC Broadcasting House, London, WlA 1AA
    Tel: 0171–580 0599
RADIO 3, BBC Broadcasting House, London, WlA lAA
    Tel: 0171–580 4468
RADIO 4, BBC Broadcasting House, London, WlA lAA
    Tel: 0171–580 4468

RADIO 5 LIVE, BBC Broadcasting House, London, WlA lAA
   Tel: 0171–580 4468
BBC World Service PO Box 76, Bush House, Strand, London WC2B 4PH
   Tel: 0171–240 3456
BBC Open University Production Centre Walton Hall, Milton Keynes
   MK7 6BH Tel: 01908-274033
BBC Enterprises Woodlands, 80 Wood Lane, London W12 OTT
   Tel: 0181–743 5588/0181–576 2000
BBC School Radio Information Officer Broadcasting House,
   London WIA IAA Tel: 0171–580 4468

BBC Scotland
BBC Radio Scotland Queen Margaret Drive, Glasgow G12 8DG
   Tel: 0141-330 2345
Broadcasting House, 5 Queen Street, Edinburgh EH2 IIF
   Tel: 0131-243 1200

BBC Wales
   BBC Radio Wales Broadcasting House, Llantrisant Road, Llandaff,
   Cardiff CF5 2YQ Tel: 01222-572888

BBC Northern Ireland
   BBC Radio Ulster Broadcasting House, Ormeau Avenue, Belfast
   BT2 8HQ Tel: 01232–244400

BBC North
   BBC North New Broadcasting House, Oxford Road, Manchester
   M60 ISJ Tel: 0161-200 2020

BBC Midlands
   Broadcasting Centre, Pebble Mill, Birmingham B5 7QQ
   Tel: 0121–414 8888

BBC South and West
   BBC Bristol and BBC West Broadcasting House, Whiteladies Road,
   Bristol BS8 2LR Tel: 0117–732211

BBC South and East
   BBC South and East Elstree Centre, Clarendon Road, Borehamwood,
   Hertfordshire WD6 IJF Tel: 0181–953 6100

Independent Radio
THE RADIO AUTHORITY
   Holbrook House, 14 Great Queen Street, London WC2B 5DG
   Tel: 0171–430 2724

ASSOCIATION OF INDEPENDENT RADIO CONTRACTORS (AIRC)
Radio House, 46 Westbourne Grove, London W2 5SH
Tel: 0171–727 2646

Audio books producers

This is a list of producers of spoken word cassettes.

Audioworks, Simon & Schuster Ltd., West Garden Place, Kendal Street, London W2 2AQ Tel: 0171–724 7577

BBC Radio Collection, BBC Enterprises Ltd., Woodlands, 80 Wood Lane, London W12 0TT Tel: 0181–743 5588

BBC School Radio Cassette Service, Broadcasting House, London W1A 1AA, answerphone service 0171–927 5821

Chivers Press Publishers, Windsor Bridge Road, Bath, Avon, BA2 3AX Tel: 01225–335336

Corgi Audio, Transworld Publishers, 61–63 Uxbridge Road, London W5 5SA Tel: 0181–579 2652

Cover To Cover Cassettes, PO Box 112, Marlborough, Wiltshire, SN8 3UG Tel: 01264–731227

Flying Dutchman Co., The, Unit 5, 143 Chatham Road, London SW11 6HJ Tel: 0171–223 9067

Harper Collins Publishers, Ophelia House, 77–85 Fulham Palace Road, London W6 8JB Tel: 0181–741 7070

Hodder Headline Books, 338 Euston Road, London NW1 3BN Tel: 0171–873 6000

Hugo Language Books, Old Station Yard, Marlesford, Woodbridge, Suffold IP13 0AG Tel: 01728–746546

Isis Audio Books, 7 Centremead, Osmey Mead, Oxford OX2 OES Tel: 01865–250333

Laughing Stock Productions Ltd., PO Box 408, London SW11 5TA Tel: 0181–944 9455

Listen For Pleasure, EMI Limited, 1–3 Uxbridge Road, Hayes, Middlesex UB4 0SY Tel: 0181–561 8722

Macmillan Audiobooks, 25 Eccleston Place, London SW1W 9NF Tel: 0171–881 8000

Mr Punch Productions, 4 Hughes Mews, 143 Chatham Road, London SW11 6HJ Tel: 0171–924 7767

Naxos Audio Books Ltd., HR House, 447 High Road, London N12 0AF Tel: 0181–346 6816

Random House Audio Books, Random House, 20 Vauxhall Bridge Road, London SW1V 2SA Tel: 0171–973 9700

Reed Audio, Reed Consumer Books, Michelin House, 81 Fulham Road, London SW3 6RB Tel: 0171–581 9393

Sound FX Audio Publishing Ltd., The Granary, Chillingloe Park, Chiddingfold, Surrey, GU8 4TA (No phone)

Soundings Ltd., Kings Drive, Whitley Bay, Tyne & Wear NE26 2JT Tel: 0191–253 4155

Speaking Books Ltd., The Chrysalis Building, 13 Bramley Road, London
    W10 6SP Tel: 0171–221 2213
Spoken Word Direct, Freepost (LV 7817), Liverpool, L70 1RN (No phone)
Talking Tape Company, Unit 11, Shaftsbury Industrial Centre, The
    Runnings, Cheltenham, Gloucestershire GL51 9NH Tel: 01242–257200
Telstar Talking Books, Telstar Records, Prospect Studios, Barnes High
    Street, London SW13 9LE Tel: 0181–878 7888

Voice Over Agencies For Commercials

Angell Sound, Garden House, 49A Floral Street, London WC2E 9DA
    Tel: 0171–333 0808
Arthur Johnson Productions, 118 Audley Road, London NW4 3HG
    Tel: 0181–202 0274
Backporch Productions Ltd., 21 Beechcroft Avenue, Hall Green,
    Birmingham B28 9ER Tel: 0121–777 9557
Big Mouth Productions Tel: 0181–997 7256
Biteback Productions, 7 Manley Road, Manchester M16 8PN
    Tel: 0161–227 9797
Black and White Radio, 15 Tenison Court, Eaton St., Norwich NR4 7BA
    Tel: 01603–502 393
Brian Lapping Associates, 21 Bruges Place, Randolph Street, London
    NW1 OTE Tel: 0171–482 5855
Broadvision, 49 Frederick Road, Edgbaston, Birmingham B15 1HN
    Tel: 0121–455 7949
Calypso Voice Over Agency, 25-26 Poland Street, London W1V 3DB
    Tel: 0171–734 6415
Commercial Works Ltd., 12 Stanhope Place, St Leonards-On-Sea, East
    Sussex TN38 OED Tel: 01424–424 474
Encore Radio, 16 Poplar Walk, London SE24 OBU Tel: 0171–733 0564
Excalibur Slack, Top Farm, Heptonstall, Hebden Bridge, West Yorkshire
    HX7 7HA Tel: 01422–843 871
Forsyth Productions, 52 Granby Road, Edinburgh EH16 5PZ
    Tel: 0131–667 9573
GRF Christian Radio, 342 Argyle Street, Glasgow G2 8LY
    Tel: 0141–221 9447
Helen Fry Productions, Old Welney Hotel, Welney, Wisbech, Cambs.,
    PE14 9TA Tel: 01354–71200
Ladbrooke Radio, Essel House, 29 Foley Street, London W1V 7LB
    Tel: 0171–323 2770
LBS Ltd., 11-13 Bamford Street, Stockport, Cheshire SK1 3NZ
    Tel: 0161–477 2710
Media Broadcast Services, 19 Cardwell Drive, Sheffield S13 7XD
    Tel: 0114–269 5461
Mediatracks, 93 Columbia Way, Blackburn, Lancs BB2 7EA
    Tel: 01254–691 197

John Mountford Studios, Heathersett, Norwich NR9 3DL
  Tel: 01603–811 855
The Soundworks Tel: 0181–441 0304
Vincent Shaw Associates, 20 Jay Mews, London SW7 2EP
  Tel: 0171–581 8215
Voice Caster Tel: 0171–624 8384
Voice Demo Services Tel: 01227–730843
Voice Shop Ltd., Bakerloo Chambers, 304 Edgware Road, London
  W2 1DY Tel: 0171–402 3966
16 Track Recording Studio Tel: 0171–381 0059

The following, costing approximately £40, supplies information on work
in voice overs and presenting, in radio and TV:
1997 Presenters Contact File, Presenter Promotions, 123 Corporation
Road, Gillingham, Kent ME7 1RG Tel: 01634–851077

The Radio Advertising Bureau is the body funded by independent radio
stations to encourage advertising:
The Radio Advertising Bureau, 77 Shaftesbury Avenue, London
  W1V 7AD Tel: 0171–306 2500

Miscellaneous

The Agents' Association, 54 Keyes House, Dolphin Square, London
  SW1V 3NA Tel: 0171–834 0515

The Community Radio Association (CRA)
  The Media Centre, 5 Paternoster Row, Sheffield S1 2BX
  Tel: 0742-795219

British Equity
  Guild House, Upper St Martin's Lane, London SC2H 9EG
  Tel: 0171–379 6000
  Conavon Court, 12 Blackfriars Street, Salford M3 5BQ
  Tel: 0161–832 3183
  114 Union Street, Glasgow G1 3QQ Tel: 0141–248 2472
  Transport House, 1 Cathedral Road, Cardiff CF1 9SD
  Tel: 01222– 397971

National Association of Hospital Broadcasting Organisations
  (NAHBO), North Bridge Tavern, 1 Frog Island, Leicester
  Tel: 0533-878409

National Association of Student Broadcasting
  Registered office, Students' Union Building, Ashby Road, Loughborough,
  Leics LE11 3TT

The Radio Academy (a professional association for those involved in radio
  broadcasting) PO Box 4SZ, 3-6 Langham Place, London W1A 4SZ
  Tel: 0171–323 3837

Index

Lightning Source UK Ltd.
Milton Keynes UK
UKOW051643100812

197341UK00001B/8/A